FENG SHUI
MODERN

FENG SHUI MODERN

CLIFF TAN
ILLUSTRATED BY DURA LEE

BLOOMSBURY PUBLISHING

LONDON · OXFORD · NEW YORK · NEW DELHI · SYDNEY

What is

1

Feng Shui?

INTRODUCTION

Let me share a little story. Some years ago, my sister bought a new flat. It was her first home, and she was excited and wanted to ensure that it was perfect. One day she asked for my opinion on which shade of purple to paint her walls. Now, my sister hates purple, and she is a pure minimalist who likes only white rooms. For her to want purple walls was nothing short of alarming. As it turned out, she had engaged the services of a feng shui master, who insisted that she paint all her walls either purple or magenta to improve her love life. But after she painted her walls these colours, her luck did not change. In fact, it got worse.

We decided to paint the walls white again, and that improved her mood and her wellbeing. She gave up on feng shui completely.

So why am I telling you this? Am I trying to say that feng shui doesn't 'work'? Not at all!

While many people see feng shui as a mysterious practice, probably because it originated a long time ago, the ideas behind it are really very simple. It is about applying common sense and instinct when you plan your spaces or build a home. There is a logical reason behind every feng shui principle. As long as we understand those principles, and apply them meaningfully to our spaces, feng shui will feel natural and instinctive, and always lead to the best possible outcomes for our homes.

So let's begin!

THIS BOOK

In this book, I aim to untangle the fundamental aspects of feng shui, and teach you how to use them in your home.

I will focus on the foundational type of feng shui, called *san he*, or the form school. This is based on the physical world – landscape, orientation, the environment and energy flow. It doesn't require any tools, just an understanding of the principles.

Feng shui can become more complex as you dig deeper into its nuances, perhaps using your date and hour of birth to calculate your lucky 'directions' and implement those in your practice. This is known as the compass school, or *san yuan*, but it's an entirely optional extension to the fundamental practice. Form school always takes priority and is often all you need to create a balanced home.

The first part of the book explains these fundamentals and how to apply them to any space. In the second half, we will look into each of the main rooms or functional spaces in our houses or apartments and decipher how best to lay them out, then how to style them to turn a house into a home. While it may be tempting to skip the foundations and launch straight in with the application of the practice, I encourage you to take a moment to really understand the founding principles. It's only through learning the ideas behind form school that you'll develop the delicate, intuitive sense necessary for a successful feng shui practice.

THE FENG SHUI STORY

Three thousand years ago in China, an emperor wished to build a new city. Not just any city – his new capital. This was a very important task, and he didn't want to get it wrong.

The first thing he needed to do was pick a site for this magnificent city. He had a team of advisors, armed with knowledge of geography and the environment, to help him decide where to put his city and in which direction it should face. They decided that, for the city to prosper, it needed to be close to a river for water and trade, at the foot of some hills to protect the houses from the wind and from enemies to the north, and on higher ground to guard against floods.

The knowledge and skills of these advisors was known as *kan yu*, which metaphorically means 'to be worthy of'. Now we call their expertise by the contemporary name *feng shui*, which simply translates as 'wind and water'.

So you see, feng shui is really just a set of theories to guide you to build something in the best possible way. The system was not unique to the Chinese. In fact, many cultures have their own rules for building, including the Indian practice of vastu shastra.

CAN FENG SHUI MAKE ME RICH AND HAPPY?

Here's the big question: does feng shui 'work'? Can feng shui improve my health, help me find a partner, or even make me rich? Let me answer this question with an analogy. If you send a child to a good school, does it guarantee that they will get a good job and become respected and rich? No, although it might help.

Like a good school, feng shui gives you the right environment in which to optimise your own performance to achieve your goals, but it cannot guarantee any specific outcome.

Just as my sister found out, spaces do shape your moods and feelings – and *this* can change outcomes. We almost always feel better in a beautiful, balanced space, and when we feel good that's already a step in the right direction to health, wealth and happiness.

Before we embark on this journey, always remember that if following a particular theory makes you feel uncomfortable, then it is not in the spirit of feng shui. Set the theory down and consider your options – let how you feel be your ultimate guide.

2

Foundations

Terms such as yin and yang, chi or the ba gua may sound mysterious, but these are nothing more than poetic descriptions of very logical ideas. In this chapter, we will decipher these terms, and dive into the foundations of feng shui.

To the Chinese, destiny is determined by three things: heaven, self and earth. The destiny from heaven refers to luck or fate, and that is out of your control. The destiny of the self is your determination and passion to achieve what you want; it originates in your mind. The destiny of earth is the environment around you and how it affects you. In other words, there is no room for superstition. Your future depends on either sheer luck (which you cannot alter), your mind and personal effort (which is completely within your control), or the environment and earth around you.

Of these, earth is physical and tangible, and you have the means to change its influence. Feng shui is all about understanding and enhancing your environment, making it as optimal as possible for your own performance in the various aspects of your life. To make the most of your environment, you need to fully grasp it.

Close your eyes, open your heart, and let's discover how the world around you was created through yin and yang. Come with me to the very beginning of time, before everything and anything, before the creation of the universe and even before thought.

There is no sky, and there are no birds, no clouds, no stars.

This is nothingness, or *wu ji*. But don't despair. Wu ji translates as 'promise', because before there was anything, there was the promise of things to come. Wu ji is represented by a perfect circle. This circle might look empty, as it represents nothing – but it is also full, and contains everything there is.

YIN AND YANG

One day, a dot appears inside this circle.

This is the seed of being, and from this comes a spark that divides the boundless circle down the middle. This split creates heaven and earth, the sky and the ground, light and darkness. These opposites are represented in the circle by one half being white, and the other, black. You can't have one without the other – you need to understand darkness before you can understand the light, and you need to see light before you can understand what is dark. This is yin and yang. For example, a glowing light bulb would be yang in a dark room, but if you compare it against the shining sun outside, it is relatively dim and yin.

This final symbol is known as *tai ji*.

In feng shui, you always need to ensure that you balance these opposites – the yin and the yang – and there can never be one without the other. Think how as the sun sets, the bright yang sunlight in a room gives way to darkness – a time when we need the yin of a soft light bulb. As a general rule, anything more subdued and calm is yin, while something with more energy is yang. These are principles that, through feng shui, we apply to create balance in the arrangement of our home and space.

16

BA GUA

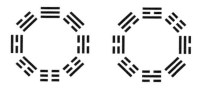

The understanding that everything is either yin or yang led to the creation of the *ba gua*, a system of solid and broken lines that appear in eight combinations of three rows, known as trigrams.

Think of yang as a solid, straight line and yin as a broken line. If you draw three solid lines stacked on top of one another, you have something wholly yang. If you draw three broken lines, you have something absolutely yin. Now, if you have two solid lines and one broken line, you have something in between – it's still yang, but with a touch of yin. If you continue to mix and match these combinations, you create a sort of binary code of yin and yang imagined as eight trigrams that are placed around a circle. This is known as the ba gua.

The position of the trigrams in the circle changes the way they interact. For example, if you place the combination of three solid lines opposite the combination of three broken lines, you achieve total balance. It's like placing fire opposite water, or black opposite white. This ba gua arrangement (above left), where opposites balance, is ordered and sensible, and is known as the 'earlier heaven sequence'.

There is another version of the ba gua, known as the 'later heaven sequence', intended to represent the real world and how relationships are not defined by opposites. In this version (above right), the locations of the trigrams are mixed up. It teaches us that a space does not always have to be perfectly balanced to be beautiful – sometimes a room that is dark with just a touch of light is all we need. This is the ba gua sequence we most commonly use in the practice of feng shui.

FIVE ELEMENTS

As we have learned, everything in the world has qualities of yin or yang, and often a combination of both. To help us understand this further, Chinese philosophy gives us five symbolic elements: fire, earth, metal, water and wood.

○ Fire represents the flame, and heat and energy.

○ Earth refers to balance and grounding.

○ Metal is known for its malleable and dense qualities.

○ Water is noted for its flowing nature.

○ Wood is seen as growth.

If we remember the yin and yang, wood and fire are yang, while metal and water are yin, and earth sits in the middle of them all, as the most balanced state.

The qualities of each element are linked to a compass direction (north, south, east and west) and season (spring, summer, autumn and winter), which is related to the environment. For example, south is represented by fire, where the sun is hottest (if you're in the northern hemisphere), and is the direction of summer.

Fire

This element burns like fire, and moves upwards like a flickering flame. It represents summer, and its direction is the south, where the sun is strongest (remembering that this is a practice founded in the northern hemisphere). The Chinese compass points south for this reason; it is where life is at its peak.

The colours that evoke fire are red and orange, and the shape is the sharply pointed triangle. Fire has no texture.

Earth

This element is subdued, like earth. Its movement is horizontal and level, like the ground. Earth has no season as it is the neutral middle, and its direction is the centre. Earth is the opposite of heaven: it is grounded.

The colours that evoke earth are yellow or brown, and the shape is the perfect square. The texture of earth is coarse and raw.

Metal

This element is malleable and condensed, like metal, but not cold or hard, and its movement is inwards like a spinning orb. It is a transformative element and so the season that it represents is autumn, and its direction is the west, where the sun sets and the day transforms from day to night.

The colour that evokes metal is white, and its shape is the evenly pressured circle. The texture of metal is shiny, viscous and smooth.

20

Water

This element is fluid, like water, and moves downwards, as gravity pulls it towards the earth. It represents winter, and its direction is the north, where the sun barely touches. This is the coolest, most fluid of the elements. Its movement is a key characteristic – it isn't still like a lake.

The colours that evoke water are black or very deep blue, and its shape is fluid and indeterminate. The texture of water is random and soft.

Wood

This element has the vitality and life of wood, and moves outwards like a tree in full growth. Its season is spring, and its direction is east, where the sun rises and breathes the most energy into the day. Contrary to the typical impression of wood, this is a living, growing element, more like a plant.

The colours of wood are green or light blue, and its shape is the vertically growing rectangle. The texture of wood is rough, like the elements of earth, but in this case the texture runs in a vertical direction, rather than a horizontal one.

ENERGY — CHI

Yin and yang and the elements represent physical things. But what of non-physical things, such as feelings, flow and energy? These are collectively known as *chi* and refer to the feelings we intuit from the world around us. Chi, which means 'air', is a fundamental concept of feng shui. It's the sense that a room feels right or not. Chi comes in different forms classified as movement, light and air, sharp edges, and ambiance. The following forms of chi are found in almost any space.

- Life (*sheng*) chi is growth, happy thoughts, a gentle breeze, plants. It breathes life into a space. This is not the same as light, and it may exist within darkness. A lush, dense forest is full of this chi. Light and air are the chi that comes from windows, sunlight, breezes. It's easy to confuse this form of chi with movement chi, especially if a room has, say, French windows, which bring both light and circulation. In this case, light, air and movement co-exist.

- Dead (*si*) chi is a stagnant stillness, like when you enter an abandoned home that has a musty smell. A space does not need to be dark to have dead chi – you can just as easily find it in a desert without any wind.

- Killing (*sha*) chi is a threatening, uncomfortable feeling, like a knife pointing towards you, and is the chi that we affect when we position our furniture. This type is directional and it affects only the person it is pointed towards. Sharp edges are physical structures within your line of sight. These may be the sharp corners of buildings, overhead beams, hanging lights or sloped ceilings (see illustration, page 25). Even though these objects have no actual impact on you, they are oppressive and have a weight. The sharpness of the angle affects the hostility of this kind of chi.

- Movement chi is about the physical circulation of chi in a space, such as through long corridors, passages and walkways. To identify how movement chi acts in any given space, you just need a floorplan that enables you to locate all the passages, corridors, stairs and high-traffic areas. Feng shui generally prefers gentle curves rather than straight lines in order to balance movement chi. Effectively, the longer a straight corridor, the stronger the chi, which is bad for a sleeping space, but good for a business. Rooms with no windows usually have no movement chi at all.

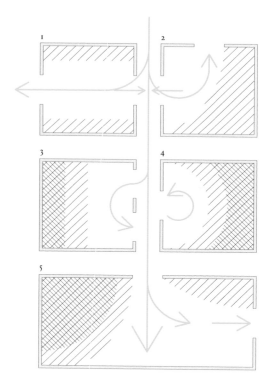

Various types of chi: The arrows show the movement of chi down a hallway and into the rooms and spaces either side. Where there are smaller arrows or none, the space is calmer and more still. The more dense the cross-hatching, the less energy is present.

→ Chi flow and circulation
▨ Areas with less energy

1   Where an entrance and exit are aligned, chi will cut through quickly
2   Chi will take a smooth and curved path from entrance to exit
3   If the entrance and exit are very close, chi will not reach deep into a room
4   Where there is an entrance with no exit, chi will not enter
5   Where a room is large, chi will cover only the areas between openings

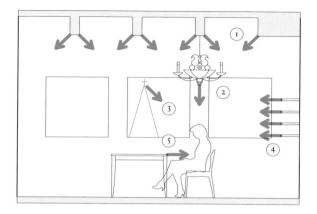

→ Aggressive, pointed elements

1 Overhead structures and beams
2 Heavy pendants or fans
3 Things that look sharp or aggressive
4 Exposed shelves
5 Corners of tables

The ambiance of a place may be created by a combination of all the types of chi, and it may depend upon a person's memories of or associations with a place. For example, a cemetery has very strong yin chi owing to its links with death. The Chinese would tend to avoid such a place, but that's not to say that some people wouldn't find a sense of peace among the dead. Many decommissioned cemeteries are now lovely parks. The point is that when you are deciding the ambiance and chi levels of a place, it really depends on how you feel about it. Other things, such as clutter, colour and the balance of the elements also affect ambiance.

Note from Cliff It's important to remember that chi cannot flow in and out of the same opening. Ideally a room should have one door and one window, on different walls.

FIVE ANIMALS

In feng shui, everything has five aspects: front, rear, left, right, centre. These are represented by the five animals: the tortoise, the bird, the dragon, the tiger and the snake. Each has a certain need you should fulfil. They aren't separate creatures hanging around you or your space, but are, in fact, a part of you and your own senses, and they influence how you react to your surroundings.

In feng shui, the five animals are most commonly used to find the command position, which we'll get to later. For now, all you need to know is that the command position is the best place to sit in a room.

Tortoise

Sometimes known as the black tortoise, this animal has links with water, and a strong shell that represents our need for stable support. The tortoise should always be behind us, protecting us — in a room, this usually means having a wall at our back. The direction of the tortoise is north, because that's the direction our back is facing when we look towards the sunny south.

Bird

Alternatively known as the vermilion bird or even phoenix, the bird links with fire and has broad wings and far-reaching sight. It asks that you have space in front of you, and ideally water (representing life). The direction of the bird is facing the south, because that is the direction of the sun.

Dragon

Also known as the azure dragon, the dragon is linked with wood, has powerful yang energy and represents our desire for growth. The direction of the dragon is to the east, where the sun rises every day and where good fortune is said to come from. The dragon is about encouraging positive energy and fresh vitality.

Tiger

Also called the white tiger, this animal is associated with metal. Its powerful body is able to protect the positive energy of the dragon, in particular.

The direction of the tiger is to the west, where the sun sets and day turns to night. Here, the tiger can detect any inconsistencies in energy, and offer balance and fortitude.

Snake

The snake is associated with earth. It has no direction – rather, it forms the central anchor for the other four animals, sitting in the middle of them. It represents our need for balance.

Essentially, the snake is your mental state and, while it is important to fulfil the requirements of the other four animals, overall wellbeing relies upon a sense of balance in mind. If something *feels* amiss in a room, even if you have fulfilled all the other requirements of feng shui, then it probably is.

How to Apply Feng Shui

3

The easiest way to get to grips with all the many aspects of feng shui is to start to apply them and see how they work in practice. So, let's begin!

THE COMMAND
POSITION

Imagine yourself sitting in a very comfortable armchair, your body leaning against a soft backrest, the arms of the chair cocooning you, and a big, open view over a majestic landscape. You feel good because all of your senses are satisfied. You are sitting in the command position, because you feel secure and at the same time in command of your space. In feng shui, we use animal symbols to represent how we should organise our space in every direction (behind, in front and to each side) in order to place ourselves in this position.

Your centre (the snake)

The snake symbolises you in the middle of a space, and how you should feel balanced on all four sides (back, front, left and right).

Your back (the tortoise)

With its hard shell, the tortoise represents protection and stability. You need this most at your back, where you can neither see nor protect yourself. A wall or a stable structure, like a high backrest, behind you positions the tortoise there. Try to avoid sitting against a window, particularly one that reaches lower than your waist, or with your back to a door, as these positions will make you feel vulnerable.

Your front (the bird)

With its wings ready for flight, the bird likes openness, and doesn't like a blocked view (say if you're facing a big wall). You need this openness in front of you, where your senses are most active, so you can see into the distance, and anticipate and plan. The tortoise and the bird work in balance – protection at your back and expansiveness in front of you.

Your sides (the dragon and the tiger)

Think back to your comfortable armchair – each of the arms is the dragon and tiger, respectively. Both have a strong inner energy – the tiger for defence and protection, and the dragon for positive growth. With your back fully protected and your front completely open, these animals offer support on either side of you. In the classical feng shui used to build houses and cities, the tortoise, dragon and tiger are manifested as hills and landforms. In practical terms, according to the principles of feng shui, you should locate your house within three hills: the highest is at the rear of the house for protection and two lower hills on either side offer support. Before you is an open view, ideally towards a body of water to signify fortune and abundance.

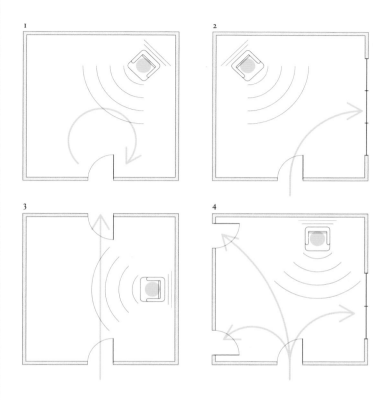

These diagrams show the command position in different rooms. Notice how the different entrances and windows affect where the command position is – even the way in which a door swings open (where it is hinged) impacts the space. The arrows represent the flow of chi through each room, which in turn affects the location of the command position.

→ Chi flow and circulation

● Best spot to be

1 Basic command position

2 Command position where there is flow of chi

3 Command position where chi cuts across and through a room

4 Command position where there are multiple openings

FLOW AND CHI

Chi is often described as the energy of a space, but what it really refers to is the feeling that you have while being in a space. Being in a command position may offer you protection, but it does not change how the space may feel around you. When we view a potential house to buy, instinctively we consider questions that, whether we know it or not, are related to chi: am I happy with the approach to the house and the entrance? What is the light like? Are there enough windows? How do I feel in the space? This chapter uses three practical scenarios to explain how chi influences us and our behaviour in a space.

THE DINING TABLE

Imagine you're at a dinner party with twenty of your friends, all seated along a very large table. You are seated at the end, at the 'head' of the table. From your seat, you can look all the way down the length and see everyone in front of you, but only the people sitting immediately to your left and right are talking to you. Despite this, though, somehow you feel like you are the centre of attention in the whole room.

THE CHANDELIER

Now picture yourself seated in the main hall of a grand, old library. There are rows of tables and chairs, and you choose to sit in the middle. What you don't notice is that the seat you've chosen is positioned directly underneath a large and heavy crystal chandelier. You sit down, then after a few minutes of reading, you look up and see the chandelier looming over you, swaying slightly. You know it's not likely to fall, but you change seats.

THE BEAST

Take yourself to the zoo, to the tiger enclosure. You have pressed your face up against the thick glass in order to look at the animals inside. All of a sudden, a tiger lunges towards you, baring its teeth and growling. You leap back. You know that the tiger can't reach you through the glass, but you don't feel safe any more, so you move on.

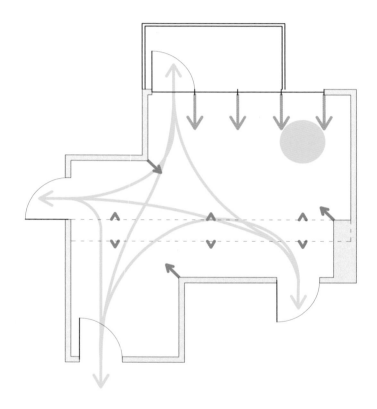

→ Chi flow and circulation
→ Aggressive, pointed elements
→ Positive energies
● Best spot to be

These three scenarios highlight different types of chi. The dining table represents movement chi, like standing at the end of a long corridor; the second shows the discomfort of being under a beam; and the final example – while a little far-fetched – shows how we dislike being confronted with sharp objects or anything that reminds us of danger.

Now that you understand what chi is, the more difficult part is how to arrange your space to maximise positive chi and minimise negative chi. After all, chi is just a feeling. Difficult as it is, there are a few core principles, and you can work out the chi of any room using a floorplan that shows all the room's structures, including the walls, doors and windows. The following exercise will help you find the positive and negative chi of a room. You'll need the floorplan of the room and three different-coloured pens or markers.

1   Use one pen to draw all the possible walking routes and circulations in the room, marking one line for every possibility. This is usually where the entrances and exits are.

2   Using a second colour, draw arrows from every sharp angle in the room, from corners of walls, edges of tables or cabinets. Don't forget to look at your ceilings for beams and fans.

3   With the third colour, consider where the windows are and where the air and natural light are coming from, and make a note of the light's strength based on the direction the window faces and the climate of the area.

4   Consider the lines on your plan. The best position for chi in this room is the space where there are no lines in the first or second colour, but where you can bathe in the light from the third set of coloured lines.

THE CAFÉ TECHNIQUE

Now that we understand both the command position and chi, here is a simple exercise to bring them together. I call it the café technique.

Imagine it is just before lunchtime, and you've arrived in a fairly empty café, planning to spend at least a few hours there. The café is spacious and located on the ground floor of the building, with large windows facing the street. Standing at one of the entrances, you look at the tables in the room — some right in front of you by the door; others located at the rear, close to the toilets; and some by the windows.

You immediately make some deductions. You do not want to sit right by the door, because it's busy and people are likely to stream in and out throughout the day. The seats by the toilets are quiet and far from the activity, but you don't really want to sit there because of the smell. You like the look of a seat close to the window as it has good light and privacy, but then you see that people are hanging around on the street outside, and can look over your back. You finally pick a seat close to a window, but with your back to a wall and with a good view of the entire room.

Despite the complex nature of this space, you made your analysis thoroughly and quickly. You looked at the flow, the potential of crowds gathering, the light levels, and also your orientation. In an instant, you were able to pick the seat that suited you best.

40

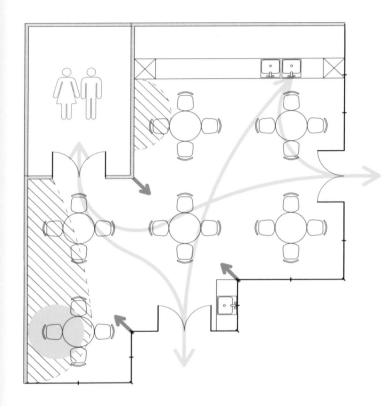

This diagram shows the tables and chairs, the various entrances, the toilets and the counter of a café and how the types of chi flow around the physical features. The calmest areas of the café are marked out in shade. The best seat in the house is the one on the lowermost left table, with its back to the wall.

→ Chi flow and circulation
→ Aggressive, pointed elements
▨ Areas with less energy
● Best spot to be

BALANCE OF
THE ELEMENTS

Now that you can identify the command position and work out the flow of chi in a room, the final step is to make your space beautiful. Doing this is not merely decorative, it goes far deeper than that. Creating beautiful space is about a methodical awareness of the environment and establishing balance so that the space not only looks nice, but feels right, too.

You should go about this in two stages. First, analyse the environment – how the natural elements affect the space. Then, look at the balance of the physical elements within the space.

The main factor that affects any environment is the sun. The kind of light that enters your home depends on where in the world you're located, which direction you're facing and, of course, the time of day.

The five elements (fire, earth, metal, water, wood; see pages 18–21) all relate to a season and a direction. Over the following pages, I've set out how the direction of your room affects your environment and its dominant element, but remember that the size of your window and whether or not there are trees or buildings outside that block the view will have their own effects. (If you live in the southern hemisphere, north is where the sun is, so simply swap the advice so that it follows north/summer and south/winter.)

North	*South*
Winter	*Summer*

North-facing rooms never receive direct sunlight. Their light is indirect, regular, calm and blue – the most neutral type of light. Imagine sunlight that has refracted through the atmosphere, distilled, and is now stable. The light here is similar to the reflected light of winter and takes a cool blue tint.

Think about the sorts of rooms that work with soft and diffused light, and don't need strong light, such as an office or studio. In these rooms, use neutral to warm tones on your walls to compensate for the cool sun, and to add yang to the space. Avoid window coverings and allow the light to freely stream in. At night, use lighting that is at the stronger end of the spectrum, to top up the lack of energy from the daylight.

During daylight hours, south-facing rooms are constantly bathed in sunlight. The light is raw and powerful, the kind that makes you want to take a siesta and seek refuge in the shade.

Public rooms, such as the living room and ideally the entrance to your home (which need light and energy), work best with such persistent light. The best colours for a south-facing room are generally vibrant, while nighttime lighting can be more ambient and soft, because there is enough light and energy during the day. If your entrance does face south, hardy plants will absorb the strong chi, and soften it.

East	*West*
Spring	*Autumn*

East is where the sun rises. Picture yourself on a cold morning, when the first rays of yellow light hit you. You will most likely feel rejuvenated and empowered. This type of light reclaims day from night, alleviating the cold with an undeniable warm energy. It is mild and cool, yet warm and powerful at the same time.

The rejuvenating light of the east is good for bedrooms or conservatories. Fill rooms facing east with wood elements (remembering that wood is about growth, so not for adult bedrooms; see page 21). While these rooms receive strong light in the morning, for the rest of the day, they will be slightly cooler. Use warmer tones for your walls and slightly stronger lighting at night.

After a long, persistent journey throughout the day, the sun retreats beneath the western horizon. The glow of the setting sun creates the most dramatic array of red and orange hues, often seeming to set the sky ablaze. This, like a tinder block, is a diminishing heat, where every drop of light becomes a precious golden leaf, fading away, paving the way for the night.

If your room faces west, it will get the richest, most orange and fiery tones. To compensate, paint your walls with cooler colours and have soft lighting for after sunset. West-facing rooms are a good choice for adult bedrooms, where things may be more passionate.

THE ELEMENT CYCLES

Now that you know about the influence of the elements over your space, you need to make sure that the elements work in balance throughout each space in your home. This section focuses on how to achieve that balance.

If there is too much or too little of one element in your space, you can use element cycles to work out how to lessen its effects or enhance the effects of the other elements to restore balance. The element cycles are a means to describe how the individual elements relate to each other. For example, we all know that water puts out fire, and so a room with lots of fire may have elements of water to dampen it; or a room with lots of browns and yellows may feel like a desert, so adding some wood elements in the form of living, green plants will mitigate it. But some things are less obvious, which is where the cycles come in particularly handy. For example, if a space is dark and cold with no sunlight, it has too much water. Instead of just adding red triangles and candles for fire and light, you could add earth-toned flooring to give it a base, some metal orbs and ornaments to bring the best out of this watery space, and wood in the form of plants to stand out beautifully against the dark backdrop.

Often shapes and colours do not correspond. You might, for example, have a tall, black triangle, which has the elements of fire and water in one. It takes some practice to read and balance these, but the main thing to remember is that the five elements are always interconnected, and where there is one, there should always be the other four. The cycles are just a means to guide you to create compositions that might have more harmony.

Finally, don't forget that your own personality will affect the overall balance of the elements in a room. Some people may have lots of fire in their character, and so a calming room might be just what they need; or someone who lives a boring life may want their space to spark fun and energy. So, not only do you need to consider the five elements, the sun/light, and the weather around you, but also think about your personality and lifestyle and how you're feeling.

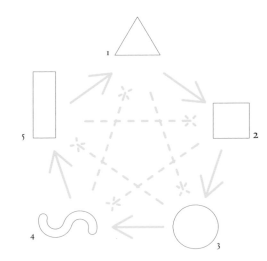

→ Creation cycles
--- Destruction cycles

1   Fire
2   Earth
3   Metal
4   Water
5   Wood

4

Planning

Now you understand the principles of feng shui, this chapter shows how you can apply them in each room of your house in a rational, considered way that suits you.

However, before we can talk about each room, we need to talk about the house itself. Remember how feng shui was used to help the emperor situate his new capital city (see page 10)? You can apply that same logic to selecting your new house or apartment.

CHOOSING
A HOME

We might not be building a capital city, but feng shui can help you pick a house, an apartment or even a room in which to live just as well. In the modern city, it's impossible to avoid compromise based on your budget, the accessibility of housing and the proximity to your work. While many of us are taught to believe that location is everything, don't sacrifice other important things for location alone. The trick is to have a list of personal and practical requirements, and order these according to priority.

I've listed the essential factors when choosing a home below. Some of them may not seem very important – but they are. Remember that while your home may be the biggest financial investment in your life, it is also the place where you spend most of your time, so in selecting a home, you should listen to both your head and your heart.

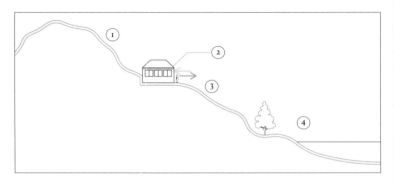

→ Chi flow and circulation
⇒ Positive energies

1 Supported from behind by a slope
2 Front door is the face of the house
3 On raised ground
4 Views towards water

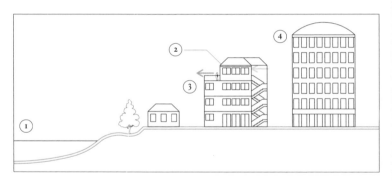

→ Chi flow and circulation
⇒ Positive energies

1 Views towards water
2 Elevated with open views
3 Main window is the face of the house
4 Taller structure behind for protection

<u>Structural soundness (or potential to be made sound)</u> Your home must be structurally safe, or, if you have found a home in disrepair, you need to have the means and ability to fix it. Be aware of leaks especially, as the most basic requirement of a home is its ability to shelter you from rain and water.

<u>Neighbourhood</u> Never underestimate the importance of the neighbourhood when you're choosing your new home. Ensure that the vital things for life – being close to parks and green spaces and clean air and water, for example – are within easy reach. Some practitioners compare roads and streets to rivers, but they are not the same: a busy road creates too much violent energy. You also want to find a neighbourhood that enables you to live within a community.

<u>Accessibility</u> Always choose a place to live that suits your needs at this point in time or the near term, rather than trying to anticipate the long-term future. Of course, this is different for everyone, so make the decision that is right for you; but don't pick a flat that isn't right, simply because it has a feature you think you might need in ten years' time.

THE COMMAND POSITION

Situating your house according to the command position means having something stable behind you. Traditionally, this would be a hill, but in a modern city it's more likely to be other buildings. To the front you need a pleasant, open view.

DIRECTION

In ancient China, houses would have their main entrance facing south, beckoning fortunes to enter. To the south is where the light is good and where crops tend to grow. Although most of us now have no crops to tend to, light is still an influence over our wellbeing.

Think of the energising, easterly morning sun, the cool stable light to the north, and the warmth of the westerly setting sun. These affect how we feel. Of course, in order to work out the appropriate orientation of your home, you need to know where its face is.

WHICH WAY DOES MY HOME FACE?

You might think that the direction your home faces is determined by the front door – but that's not always the case, particularly if you're living in an apartment, a dorm or a shared house. The simplest method for working out which way your home faces is to *feel* the strongest feature of your house, whether that's a door or a window. The direction that you feel your home faces is usually right.

Front door   This is usually only for houses, where the door forms the main impression of your home.

Main window   In an apartment, select the largest window or collection of windows, which are the main source of light and energy. If you're renting a room in a house or apartment, the 'face' of your home may be either the window of your bedroom or your room's door, depending upon where you get most of your energy.

54

ENTRANCE

A beautiful entrance is key to creating a good feeling when you come home every day, and will bring good fortune and energy.

THE MAIN DOOR

The main door is the mouth of your house, where all things enter – good or bad, feelings or fortunes; where the outside world comes into contact with your world. It is a symbolic feature of your home that we need to treat with respect. For visitors, it is the first experience of your home, and you want it to make a good impression – even if you don't often have guests, you want it to impress yourself!

Quite simply, the main door is the door you use most to enter your home – and that might be at the front or the back of the house. It can also be different from the door that was originally intended – some people use their patio or utility-room doors more than their actual front door. The rule is the door that you use most is the main door to your home, and you should treat it as such.

THE ENTRANCE

Now that you've worked out the main door of the house, think about what's around the entrance.

○ Celebrate the entrance! There's only one chance to make a first impression, so ensure there's lots of light and energy around your main entrance, as that will make it feel more welcoming. If your door faces a back street or dark alleyway or corridor, decorate it to make it feel positive (see pages 57–9). Upon entry, ensure that there is some space to take in your home, such as a hallway or entry area (see pages 60–61). If you live in an apartment block, while the doors of the complex aren't your main door, they are still important. There is little you can do to personalise the communal entrance, but try to be aware of the guiding principles of position, orientation, energy and light and do what you can to optimise them. Consider the entire approach, through the corridors, in the lift, and up to your actual front door.

○ The approach should not be 'aggressive'. A long, straight path or corridor that leads directly to your door introduces aggressive chi that rushes towards you. Much like the length of a blade, the length of the road also determines the weight of the chi. Try to create scenarios outside the house to dampen the effect – sometimes simply meandering the shape of the path that leads to your door with carefully placed pot plants or shrubs is all you need. If you live in an apartment, don't worry – you can dampen the effects from the inside.

○ The door should always lead to a public area of the house, not the private area, especially if you usually use a side door to enter your home. If, in your house, the bedrooms are around the entrance and the living room is at the rear, lead the eye to the back of the house, past the private areas. Do this by closing the bedroom doors at all times, and camouflaging them (for example, paint them in the same colour as the hallway walls).

○ In apartment buildings, sometimes the doors of two apartments may face each other directly, which can feel confrontational and awkward. There's an easy way to fix this: simply declare this space a shared area, and invite your neighbour to help you decorate it with some plants or something similar.

THE DOOR

Your main door should look strong and imposing – and welcoming.

Colour

Depending on the direction that your door faces and its immediate surroundings, the colour you choose for it can create balance or imbalance. For example, if your door faces north or there is little light, paint it black or the colour of water so that it blends in. If it faces south or is very sunny and bright, a red door would bring out this strong energy. Remember also the colour of your door creates an impression of what to expect within your home.

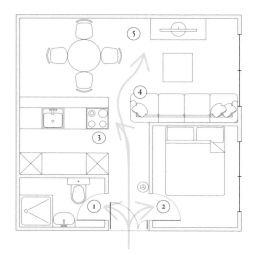

BAD

→ Chi flow and circulation

1 Toilet visible from entrance
2 Bed is the first thing you see
3 Stove within sight
4 Furniture blocking the way
5 Nothing to draw the eye

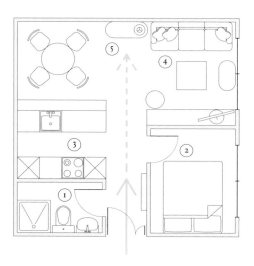

GOOD

→ Chi flow and circulation
⇢ Chi is weakened

1 Toilet located out of sight,
 even close up
2 Bed in a private position
3 Stove out of sight
4 View of comfortable sofa to
 set the tone
5 Focal point to draw the eye

58

Entry mat

First and foremost, never choose a door mat that displays the logo or symbol of something you respect – as you will trample all over it! However, if you're drawn to a mat with a playful image of something you love, or a joke, be guided by your instincts and interpret the guidelines in a way that suits your nature.

Flow

Doors should open inwards to encourage an inward flow of chi.

Size and proportion

As the mouth of the home, the door should be proportionate to your home's scale, while at the same time being more prominent than any other door in the house or apartment. A door that's too small can mean that less fortune will enter your home. A door that's too big won't be able to hold your fortune, or could mean that you're not modest. If you're using a side door to enter the house, decorate it with plants on either side, or create a welcoming path leading up to it, to make it obvious that this is the entrance.

Material

Choose a main door that's made of solid wood (the correct element for a door). Glass windows in your doors represent fragility – you want your doors to be strong and sound to symbolise security.

It's worth noting here that French doors are not considered doors, but windows. So, if you access your home through the garden and French doors are your entry point, change them to solid doors.

HALLWAY OR ENTRY AREA

Your entry space provides a first impression of the interior of your home and sets its tone. It is also a place where you can soften any strong chi from the outside. Treat your hallway like a full room and give everything its proper place – don't just throw shoes about in it! Even if you don't have an actual hallway, give the entrance area behind the front door a sense of identity and importance.

○ If your front door is at the end of a long corridor or pathway with lots of chi, and you can't change the outside, create chi absorbers. Screens or pendant lights within the hallway will prevent rushing energy penetrating your house. Make sure you don't completely deflect the chi, though – avoid placing a mirror directly opposite the door.

○ Always keep your entry space bright and well lit so that you feel the celebration of returning home.

○ Add broad-leaf plants. These have a wonderful energetic yang effect, which reminds you that your home is a place where life thrives. Make sure your hallway has lots of natural light so that any plants can survive.

○ Place any religious artefacts, or altars or shrines in your entry space to remind you of your guides and inspirations every time you return home.

○ Keep the hallway open and spacious without obstacles to allow for a smooth entry.

○ Avoid sharp corners or beams, including open shelves, over or around the entry area. If you can't avoid this, paint them the same colour as the walls to make them less obvious, or soften them with plants or lights.

○ If your front door leads straight through your home into the living space, place a screen or table of flowers to divert the flow of chi, so that it does not rush into your home.

60

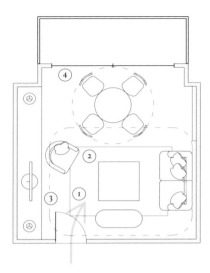

→ Immediate entry area

1 Entry straight into living space
2 Awkward squeeze to access dining area
3 Anyone entering will immediately see the TV
4 Views to the outside are blocked, chi cannot flow

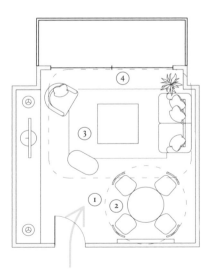

GOOD

→ Immediate entry area

1 An entry space to pause and take in the entire room
2 Dining area close to entry point
3 Living space separate from entry area
4 Views out of the room are maintained

○ No brooms, mops and bins. Keep these hidden from the entry area or as discreet as possible.

NARROW ENTRANCES

Very often, your front door will open straight into a long, often dark corridor. Try to make this space as bright as possible.

○ Place a mirror on the side wall to give a sense of width (never place it on the end wall, which reflects the chi out of the house).

○ Put bright vibrant artworks on either side of the corridor to draw attention away from the length and slow down the rush of chi.

○ If the corridor is too tight for furniture or artwork, hang an attractive pendant light, giving something for visitors to enjoy.

○ If you have private rooms adjacent to the door, or if your entryway is tight and unpleasant, try to lead people's attention past this and straight into the more public rooms at the end. Place a focal point at the end of the room, such as a sculpture, shrine, piece of furniture, or lamp (it doesn't have to be something useful, it can just look nice as its purpose is to lead you in).

NO ENTRYWAY

Some apartments don't have a hallway – but an entry space is vital for adjusting your mood as you enter your home. Try to create one.

○ If your door opens straight into a living room, try to arrange your furniture so that it almost forms a circle, in a way that suggests a hallway area near the entry.

○ If your door opens straight into a kitchen, keep the kitchen tidy at all times and hide or disguise all functional items, such as the fridge. It's okay to display beautiful bowls of fruit, but not boxes of half-eaten cereal! If you don't have storage space, try to place the negative items so that they can't be seen as you enter the room. Most importantly, make sure that people can't see the oven and hob.

○ If your entrance opens into a dining room, ensure there is a clear path from the entrance to the rest of the home: do not block the entrance with the dining table. Avoid placing seats with their backs to the door.

STAIRCASES

Like a corridor, having a staircase at the entrance of your home invites strong chi. The effect of chi is more intense in a stairway – stairs heading upstairs carry more energy, and stairs leading downstairs take energy away. Both impact the feng shui of a home, usually in a negative way. The best way to mitigate the effect of a staircase facing the door is either by placing a screen in front of it, or by turning the last two steps so that the staircase does not face the door. Alternatively, draw attention from it by hanging a statement pendant light to draw the eye upwards.

LIVING
ROOM

The living room is the most important room in the house. It's the anchor, the place where family members gather. It's usually the largest room, and the first place you bring visitors, making it the room with the most life and positive chi.

LOCATION

If you're designing your own house, the living room should be in the middle of the home, in sight of all the other rooms.

FEELING AND PLAN

The living room is flexible and can have many functions. The first thing to establish is how you want to use your living room, but one general rule is that it should feel inviting. The most common pieces of furniture in a living room are chairs or sofas. These should face each other to show that it's a communal space, and to encourage interaction. Don't let the TV take centre stage. Furthermore, in this room, everyone is welcome – so make sure there are enough seats for all the people who live in your house, as well as for guests.

The living room is a place with lots of energy, so decorate it with lively adornments, such as plants, mirrors and even an aquarium. When hanging mirrors, position them to reflect the lovely things in the room. Avoid reflecting the doorways.

THE SOFA

The main seat – usually a sofa – in the living room should take the command position. To decide where to place your sofa, consider the principles of the five animals: there should be a wall behind it and space in front of it, and you should be able to see the entrance to the room when you sit on it. Watch out for excessive chi – the sofa should not be in line with a corridor, or have beams directly above it.

○   Ideally, have one main sofa, with armchairs to complete the arrangement.

○   Two sofas facing each other across an empty space is confrontational and formal, so place a coffee table between them to soften the tension.

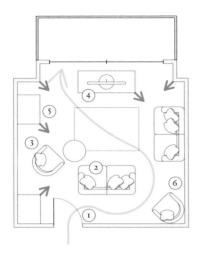

BAD

→ Chi flow and circulation

→ Aggressive, pointed elements

1   Constricted entry makes it hard to enter
2   Sofa not in command position
3   All seats are facing the TV
4   TV is in the most prominent position
5   Exposed corners from floating furniture
6   Lone chair (out of the social 'circle') signifies an unwelcome guest

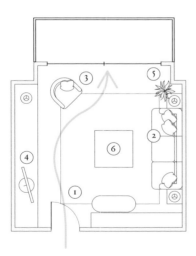

GOOD

→ Chi flow and circulation

1   Open entry allows chi to meander in without being too direct
2   Sofa is generous and in command position
3   Seats form an enclosed social circle
4   TV is placed discreetly and out of sight from entry
5   Exposed corners are filled with furniture or softened by plants
6   Prominent coffee table to anchor room

- An L-shaped sofa forms an incomplete social circle. Place an armchair or two diagonally from the corner of it.

- If you can't place the sofa against a wall and it needs to float in the room, have a low console table behind it to offer rear protection, or opt for a sofa with a thick back rest or one that is firmly grounded on the floor.

- If your living room has sloped ceilings, try to avoid placing the sofa under the low end. If this is where the command position is, place lights on either side to 'push' the ceiling upwards.

- Don't leave your sofa alone! Complement it with an armchair, a bench or a statement stool.

OTHER FURNITURE

Armchairs An armchair is a supporting piece to the sofa – it helps complete the social circle of the living room. It does not need to be in the command position, as it's for a guest to sit on, or there to demarcate a space. The exception is if your main seat is the armchair and the sofa is for guests. In that case, give the armchair priority for the command position over the sofa. Face your armchair towards the sofa – you don't want all of your seats facing the same direction.

Coffee tables Place a coffee table in the centre of a room to anchor the space and unify the separate seats. A living room without a great coffee table is just floating around a void! Coffee tables also help to separate chairs and mediate conversations, softening a confrontational, formal setting – of two sofas facing each other, say. As a significant piece of furniture, your coffee table should be decorated with something beautiful and lively to suggest surplus and prosperity.

Side tables These expand the scale of small sofas, making them feel wider and more generous. If you can't have a coffee table in your living room, ensure you have a side table.

Television Few of us want to admit that a TV is more important to us than our friends, but it is nonetheless a fundamental of most living rooms. Show that convivial interaction is a priority over the TV by shifting it from the centre of the room to a less significant corner. Always place your TV as low as possible – avoid hanging it high on a wall. If you can't place it in a corner, try putting it on a large cabinet, with the TV at one end, and a lamp at the other to balance out the weight of the TV. Another trick is to have a TV on legs and place it in a corner of the room, much as you would place a stool or armchair. Never place a TV over a fireplace as that position will give it too much significance.

Sideboards or cabinets These are not only functional as they provide storage, but will help your space feel lived-in. Place decorative objects, such as a TV (see above) or lamp strategically on them to enhance your space. Adding a tall accessory adds height. Cabinets also give a good base over which to hang pictures.

Mirrors While the living room is an energetic place, making it a good place to hang mirrors, be aware of what you reflect. Do not have a mirror that reflects the TV or doorways. A good rule is to place mirrors where you would otherwise like to have windows.

Lighting Create depth in your living room using many different light sources. If you must have a chandelier, never place it over the sofa or other seating positions. Try it over the coffee table.

Small living rooms

Don't fight against your space – a small room is cosy, don't try to do too much with it.

○ Have fewer but larger pieces, like one double sofa instead of two armchairs, or a long console instead of a row of cabinets.

○ Go large with objects that don't take up floor space. Think big lighting or a statement artwork, as these add scale. Similarly, try floor-to-ceiling curtains.

○ Ensure that seating and walking spaces are generous – don't block access and don't clutter seats.

○ Rugs bring scale without compromising on space, but make sure they're large enough to go under half of all furniture in the room.

Long living rooms

Chi tends to flow too quickly in long rooms, so place objects to regulate it and help it meander.

○ Place furniture across the width of the room, rather than lengthways.

○ Place large, arresting artworks on the long walls – they act like windows to expand the width.

○ Mirrors expand a narrow space, but don't have too many, and most especially, don't place a mirror at the end of the room.

○ Position a statement piece, be it art or a piece of furniture, at the end of the long room to make the room seem a little shorter.

○ Place the things you use the most close to the front of the room.

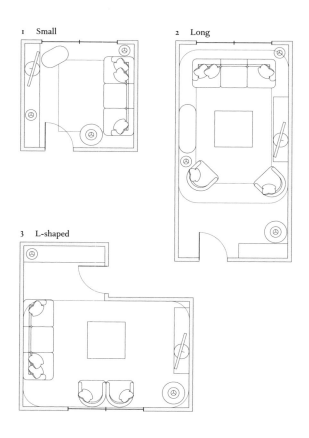

1 Small

2 Long

3 L-shaped

Irregular and L-shaped living rooms

Don't worry about trying to make a living-room space look more regular than it is, as it is a flexible room. Instead, the goal is to soften irregular corners rather than closing them off.

- Expand the room using mirrors to reflect the space.

- Make good use of every alcove for supportive functions, like reading nooks, as long as the central area is clear and regular.

- Avoid placing seating in an alcove that is separate from the main area, as this suggests people are being left out.

Living rooms with too many windows and doors

As living rooms are transitory spaces, they sometimes have doors leading to other rooms. Here's how to anchor the space.

- Have a strong focus such as a large coffee table with a statement piece on it to draw attention away from the doors around.

- If you have to place the sofa against windows, ensure the windows start higher than the height of the sofa, or place something behind it – you should not be able to see the back of a sofa from outside.

- If the space is large enough, create walkways around the back of the seating and sofa.

- If the space is small, position the sofa where the doors and windows are least accessed.

- If you need to have a pathway through the room, ensure it goes around the seating arrangement.

DINING ROOM

While the living room might be the most important room in the house, the dining room or dining area comes a close second, and should never be an afterthought. It is the heart of the home, as it brings friends and family together.

In many modern homes, we have incorporated the dining area into an open-plan kitchen. In small homes, we may have disguised it as a foldable table that we can stow away. In some stately homes, the dining room is a showpiece, used only once or twice a year on special occasions. The key is to bring the right balance of presence and function to this space.

72

LOCATION

Try to place the dining room at your home's centre, not too close to the entrance, nor in view of the main door, where it will get too much chi. Ideally, the dining room will be visible before the private areas of the house, and, if your home has several levels, it should be on a level lower than the bedrooms – but not in the basement, if possible. If you can't position your dining room centrally, try to suggest a central position by placing mirrors to expand the space to the off-centre side, or decorate the room symmetrically with a striking pendant or light.

For practical reasons, keep your dining room next to your kitchen. The path between the two rooms is always high traffic, so make sure pathways are clear and accessible.

If there is a room between the kitchen and dining room (such as the living room), make sure there's a dedicated route between them.

FEELING AND PLAN

Like the living room, the dining room likes lots of energy, and needs sunlight and air. However, if you have to choose between having your dining room close to a kitchen, or having it in a room with lots of windows, always prioritise the kitchen.

○ Place the dining table in the centre of the room and make it the focus. Then, look at the placement and the positioning of the dining chairs. Will everyone be comfortable? Is there enough circulation around the space?

○ As the dining room is the heart of the home and needs to be balanced, it is represented by the earth element. Keep the features, fixtures and fittings in this room earthy and neutral. If you use a stronger colour palette throughout the rest of your home, ensure the tones aren't as strong in this room.

○ You want your dining room to be bright and energetic. Hang a beautiful pendant lamp or chandelier above the table to draw people in. Usually, this is the only place in the home that really requires a pendant light.

○ Hang mirrors in the dining room to reflect good food and happy times. As always, don't hang a mirror so that it reflects the doorway. Instead, aim to reflect the table. And use complete mirrors that do not distort reflections and can capture a person fully. It's great to hang artwork in happy, vibrant colours on the walls of a dining room – maybe even show some enticing images of food.

○ You want to showcase abundance in the room, so the dining table and other sideboards should never be empty. Always have something on the table, such as fruit or flowers. It's great to have plants in the dining room, as long as there's enough light for them to flourish.

○ Avoid clocks, which can create a feeling of haste when we should be focusing on company and conviviality.

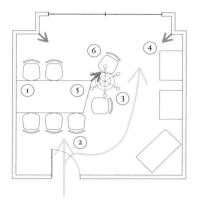

BAD

→ Chi flow and circulation

→ Aggressive, pointed elements

1　Table is pushed off-centre against wall
2　Seats are directly at the entrance
3　Pendant light hangs over seats
4　Floating furniture and exposed corners
5　Irregular-shaped table with a sharp corner
6　Odd number of chairs and bad positioning around the table

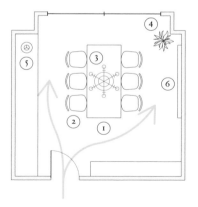

GOOD

→ Chi flow and circulation

1　Table is in the middle of the room
2　No seat is in a vulnerable position
3　Pendant hangs centrally over table
4　Plants soften corners and bring yang energy
5　Console to support the dining function
6　Mirror to reflect food and happy moments

DINING TABLE

The dining table is the most important piece of furniture in the dining room. Position it in the centre of the room with a good view of the entrance, but not in its way.

Command position

Unlike a sofa or bed, the dining table has no command position – the idea instead is to allow as many people as possible to be in their own command positions while sitting around the table. If the dining table is in the middle of the room, then everyone will have a good view of everyone else. Nevertheless, in every dining setting, there are good and bad seats. Always offer the best seats to the main guests or most senior or most respected people. The worst seat is usually the one closest to the entrance to the room, which has its back to the door. This is where the most junior guest, or the host, will sit (although some people place their rivals in these seats).

Don't place a dining table against a wall – ensure that there's flow around the table, and that you won't have to squeeze people in. You would also want to avoid people sitting facing a wall.

Table shape

Choose a dining table that is a regular shape and that's the right size for your level of entertaining – tables that are too big and always empty create imbalance.

- Circular tables are best, as they do not have any sharp corners and hierarchy is based on orientation, rather than who is sitting at the ends.

- Oval tables are the next best shape.

- Square tables are good as they represent the earth element, which corresponds to the dining room.

- ○ Rectangular tables are acceptable but take note of the command position, and bear in mind who sits on the ends, at the 'heads'.

- ○ Avoid irregular-shaped tables or abutting different tables together. Your dining table should feel unified and whole.

Table material

Wood is ideal for a dining table, as it represents the earth element. Similarly a stone table is good, or even a clay or terracotta table. Avoid glass, as this makes the space feel busy, and it can be disconcerting to see people's legs while you're eating. But if that's what you have, place a tablecloth over it when you're entertaining.

Dining chairs

The dining chairs determine the mood of the room. To ensure fairness, all chairs should look exactly the same, which will avoid any notion of hierarchy. Use chairs that look solid and stable. Low-backed chairs look more relaxed and laid back, whereas high chairs make a dining room feel more formal.

- ○ Always have an even number of chairs at the table, without placing any of them at the corners. Make sure they are comforting and welcoming.

- ○ Temporary-looking, plastic chairs make your space look like a school canteen or hostel. Avoid them if you can, but otherwise ensure they are comfortable and feel stable.

- ○ Keep spare chairs away from the room – left on the side of the dining room or around the table, they signify unwelcome guests.

OTHER FURNITURE

Consoles and side tables are there to support the main dining table. Place them to the side of the room, against the walls (the only furniture in the centre of the room should be the table and chairs). Make sure they don't tower or loom too much over the dining table.

CHALLENGING ROOM SHAPES

Small dining rooms

○ Have a smaller table and large, generous chairs with arms to make the room feel more generous, as well as comfortable.

○ If you need to seat more people, have smaller chairs without arms, but keep the backs low to make the space feel bigger. In this case have a more beautiful table to compensate.

○ If the ceilings are high enough, hang a large pendant in the small room to bring up the scale without encroaching into the space.

○ Add mirrors, which will make a small room feel larger.

○ Resist the urge to go small with everything – a large artwork and tall table piece will make the space feel larger. Try not to place the table against a wall, or, if you do, place a mirror on that wall so the table doesn't feel 'terminated'.

Long dining rooms

○ Try to use oval tables instead of long, rectangular tables to slow down chi. These also look wider while not taking more space.

○ Use chairs with arms, as this creates intervals between seats.

○ Avoid using long benches.

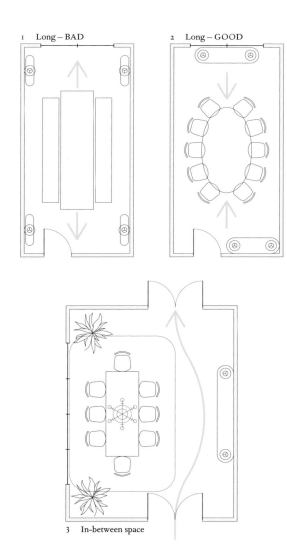

1   Long – BAD

2   Long – GOOD

3   In-between space

→   Chi flow and circulation

- Place mirrors on the long walls to widen the room, but avoid placing them at the ends of the room.

- If the room is very long and you don't need a large table, try a smaller table and leave an empty space at either end of the room for a console and other supporting furniture.

- Place large, arresting artworks on the long walls, as they act like windows and expand the width of the room.

Irregular and L-shaped dining rooms

- Place furniture or plants strategically to soften the irregular shape.

- If the room has nooks and crannies, give these a function. For example, make them a drinks area or even a break-out space. The main dining table should feel central.

Dining rooms in alternative spaces

- Avoid rooms that have no windows at all.

- Avoid positioning your dining room in transitory spaces, such as a hallway. But, if your dining space is in a hall area, place consoles around the table to anchor the space.

- Ensure there are generous walkways around the table, wherever you place it.

- If the dining room has to be located in an in-between space – for example, between the rest of the house and the kitchen – ensure there is a clear path around it.

- If you need to place the table off-centre to create a wider walkway, create focus with a pendant light hung centrally over the table.

- If the dining table is in line with the main door to your home, place a console to protect it (relevant only for main doors).

KITCHEN

Feng shui traditionally viewed the kitchen as a service room that wasn't a part of the home. It was considered to have a disproportionate influence from the element of fire. Of course, over time this has changed, and feng shui itself now needs to catch up — but that's okay! Modern kitchens have better insulation, and they perform better than they did in the past, reducing the impact of fire. More importantly, kitchens often now take on the role of social spaces, where the family may gather to cook together and share happy times. In addition, how we use a kitchen influences the effects of fire. If you're making cold food, and not 'cooking' at all, fire is less prominent, or even non-existent, so bear these scenarios in mind when reading, and adapt these guidelines for how you use your space.

LOCATION

Regardless of how its functions evolve, the kitchen will always be the source of food and therefore represents inner wealth. As a result the kitchen should have a place of its own rather than being tucked into a transitory space between rooms.

○ The kitchen should not be the centre of the home as there is too much fire in it. If yours is, push the focus to the neighbouring dining area.

○ Ideally, your kitchen should be in the rear half of your home, further from the entrance, which is more for living areas. If your kitchen is open plan, locate it at the rear part of the main room.

○ If your kitchen is close to your main entrance, avoid being able to see it, particularly its stove, from the front door, as the fire will burn away the good chi that enters the house.

○ The strong fire element of the kitchen means you shouldn't have rooms that have a strong water element nearby. For example, avoid having a toilet that faces the kitchen. Or, if you do, keep the doors closed.

○ Keep your kitchen away from your bedrooms – avoid placing a bedroom next to and especially over the kitchen. Keep the bed away from the heat of the stove, if you live in a studio.

○ If your kitchen is also your dining room, it becomes a place of gathering and takes on the role of a dining room. In this case, you can give it more attention, but because of its strong affinity to the fire element, you should still avoid using mirrors or anything that evokes the water element.

○ The kitchen should have natural ventilation, so place it where there are windows nearby.

The main cooking appliance – such as the stove – should always be the central element of the room, and the sink should be secondary. Avoid placing them next to one another. Next, decide where the other big items – such as a fridge or dishwasher – should go. You'll want lots of working space, but this is better on an island.

Principles to follow

○ Keep the fire and the water elements apart. If the stove and sink or fridge are next to or opposite each other, place wood – such as plants – between them to mediate.

○ Keep the kitchen tidy at all times, especially if it is visible from the entrance. Never leave dirty dishes out, and try not to leave them in dishwashers for too long before cleaning them.

○ The kitchen is a yang area of the house and needs windows to allow chi to enter, and good ventilation and natural light.

Situations to avoid

○ Avoid introducing the water element into the kitchen (a place of fire). If you want to paint the room in a neutral, water tone, balance it out with earth.

○ Knives signify aggression. Keep them inside drawers, out of sight.

○ Keep exposed shelves to a minimum. They produce aggressive chi and also lead to cluttered-looking spaces.

○ Do not have mirrors in the kitchen – they will reflect the kitchen's aggressive chi around the space. Particularly don't have a mirror facing the stove or hob.

○ Avoid having bins and recycling containers on display.

1 Dine-in kitchen with units
   to one side
2 Galley kitchen with clashing
   elements separated
3 Large kitchen with island and
   with the stove in the command
   position

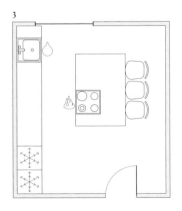

STOVE

Command position

Traditionally, the stove or oven is the most important item in the kitchen, and therefore it takes the command position. Place it at the rear of the space, away from the door or entrance and not directly facing it, but always in view.

Equivalent appliances

Anything that cooks and produces heat, such as a toaster or microwave, is a source of fire. If you use any of them more often than a stove, these become the main source of fire.

Ovens As you do not need to attend to an oven while your food is cooking, the command position is not so important. However, be aware that ovens emit the fire element from the front. Keep your oven away from seating areas.

Hobs Food on a hob requires constant attention, so place your hob so that you can command the kitchen appropriately. If cooking is a lifestyle event for you, place it on a deep island, so that when you cook you're facing the rest of the kitchen and not the wall. If cooking is an intensive, solo activity, face the backsplash and the wall. Avoid putting a hob under a window, as it means energy will leave the space; the hob should either face the island, or the wall with a backsplash.

OTHER ITEMS

Sink

○   Keep the sink or any other appliance strong in the water element away from the stove, or at least have a gap between the two.

- The kitchen is meant to be a warm, fiery place, so keep the sink discreet.

- The sink may be under a window or in a kitchen island as it does not need support.

Fridge

- The fridge is a water appliance, so avoid placing it next to the cooker. If you do, ensure there is good insulation between the two.

- The fridge is not something to celebrate, so try to choose one in a colour that blends in with the kitchen, or even hide the fridge completely by using an integrated type.

Other appliances

Treat all other appliances that use water, including dishwashers and washing machines, as you treat the fridge, and keep them away from the appliances that are heavily influenced by fire.

CHALLENGING ROOM SHAPES

Small kitchens

- Ensure you have the basics in your kitchen, using dual-purpose appliances, such as a combination oven/microwave, if you can.

- Choose smaller appliances, such as a two-ring hob, but ensure they are fit for your use.

- Integrate! Integrated appliances make the room feel calmer and more cohesive, which gives a sense of space.

- Keep the space tidy at all times. While this is important regardless of the size of your kitchen, it is essential for smaller spaces.

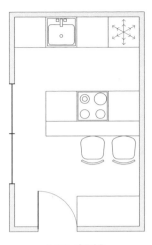

Long – BAD

Galley with inaccessible fixtures

Long – GOOD

Galley with a more square layout
and fixtures within reach

○ If you have ample storage for your needs, go without overhead cabinets, which can make small kitchens feel more oppressive.

Long kitchens

○ A long space makes for a good galley kitchen. If you need to fit a breakfast table in there too, fit the cabinets horizontally with a small peninsula.

○ Hang wide pendant lights and avoid hanging lines of little pendants, which might make the room feel like a carriage.

○ Push appliances to the end wall, and have a generous island in the middle for preparing food.

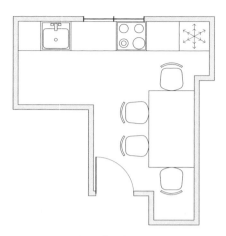

Irregular – BAD

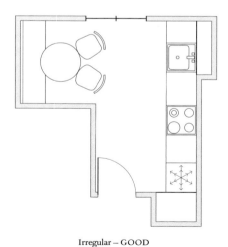

Irregular – GOOD

Filled awkward corners

Irregular and L-shaped kitchens

○ Close up awkward niches and corners by building larders or pantries, which will also free up storage space in the kitchen.

○ Fit large items like your fridge inside corners.

○ In an L-shaped kitchen, keep all the working elements within sight of each other. If there is a corner far from everything, use it as a large larder or breakfast area.

Rooms with no windows

○ Open up the space more – so that energy can flow easily in and around it.

○ Use more side lighting to create a lighter, more energised feel. It's tempting to use mirrors to make a space feel bigger, but avoid having them in the kitchen.

OFFICE

If you apply properly the principles of feng shui to your work area, your efforts will literally pay off! The command position really matters in an office space, because this is a room where you concentrate and make a living and you need the best environment to perform to the best of your ability.

LOCATION

The location of a workplace in your home is not as straightforward as the other functions: what you need from the space depends upon your type of work, and the environment you need in order to flourish.

○ If your work needs peace and protection, especially if you need to focus, make your office at the rear of your home, where things tend to be calmer.

○ If your work is about connecting with the public, and about reputation and rapport, create an office at the front of your home, closer to the higher activity areas.

○ Keep your work space away from other service areas with irrelevant functions, such as the kitchen and bathroom. Of course, if your work is about cooking, this is an exception.

○ Even if you work in the living room or bedroom, make a distinction between the functions of the space, to keep them as separate and distinct from one another as possible.

○ If you need to work at the dining table, see pages 126–7.

FEELING AND PLAN

The office should always have plenty of light, both natural and artificial. It's always best to work in daylight, so choose a room with windows. This will also bring good chi, which needs to enter and exit a room from different openings – in this case the door and window.

The most important space in your office will be the space you work at, where you spend most of your time. Always place this in the command position and so that you face the door.

Entrance If clients visit you in your office, ensure that the entry is welcoming and distinctive, which will suggest that customers and wealth can easily find you.

<u>Colours and elements</u> Make sure these match the aspirations of your business. If you want growth, choose greens and light blues; if you want wealth, use rich tones such as gold; and if you want stability, use earthy, neutral tones. If your business is fluid and versatile, black or dark blues are appropriate. If it is precise and pristine, choose white.

<u>Art and graphics</u> These can be powerful motifs and should symbolise your work and positive growth. Avoid hanging portraits in your office, as faces can intimidate – unless, of course, they inspire you.

<u>Lighting</u> Unlike in the rest of your home, opt for even, bright lighting in your office.

<u>Order</u> Keep the space neat and tidy at all times, unless you have a very specific system. Even then, always categorise your work and documents sensibly so you won't forget where you've put things, should you need them again.

<u>Plants</u> An office is a yang area, so it's good to feature plants in it. Place your plants where they will get natural light from your window.

<u>Aquariums</u> An aquarium is said to bring wealth and energy, which makes it a good addition to your office – as long as you look after it!

DESK

Command position

The desk, or other type of work furniture (whether that's a table, sewing machine, piano, or even an easel) is where you spend most of your time in this space. Position it so that you are in the command position when you're working. Have a wall behind you so that nobody can see you from the back, and never have your back to the door. From where you sit, you should be able to see the door. Avoid sitting under a beam or having a pendant light directly over your head or desk.

○ If you can't achieve the command position, it's fine to have your side facing the door, just not your back.

○ Chi comes in through doors, so avoid sitting too close to the one that opens into your office.

○ Ideally have the window to your side to give a pleasant, even light to your work space. Try not to have a window behind you, as it gives the feeling of being watched. Neither should you face a window, as it would become a distraction, while also giving glare.

○ Ensure you have an easy pathway, free from obstacles, to your desk or other workstation.

○ If your work setup has many computers and screens, it's better to face a wall. The screens act as windows to the outside world. Just be sure that if you're facing a wall, you don't have wall-mounted shelves looming over you and you're still able to see the door.

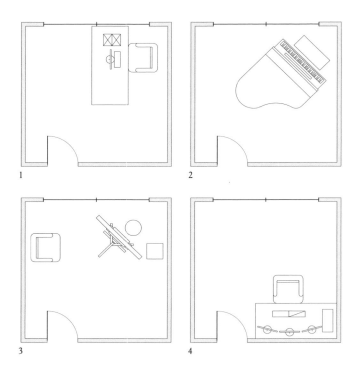

The command position relates to the person, not the furniture. The ideal office setup is when you are in a command position with most of the room and the door in front of you. An open space in front of you gives good foresight and allows wealth and fame to come. Behind you, opt for a solid wall for stability and protection, where you can place your bookshelf to represent your career, knowledge and mentors. In the middle of the room, you represent your own balance and wellbeing. Remind yourself of why you work, with pictures of family or whatever gives you peace by your side.

1 Command position of a normal writing desk
2 Command position for a grand piano – the piano's back is to the door
3 Command position of an easel – the back of the canvas faces the door
4 Command position of a desk with many screens, which need to be against a wall

Desk shape and material

○ Rectangular desks are for hard negotiating.

○ Curved desks are for creativity.

○ Reflective surfaces bring too much energy.

○ Light- or natural-coloured desks are best.

Bookshelves and storage

○ Try to avoid open shelves, which give off aggressive chi.

○ More important than its location, a bookcase needs to be easily accessible and within reach from where you work.

○ Keep things arranged and sorted so that you will be able to easily locate documents or references that you need.

○ Keep your books upright on your shelves. Books that have been laid on their side are hard to take down and they make an office look cluttered.

○ If you are an artist or creative person who uses tools, store them so that you can easily reach them.

○ As a rule of thumb, keep reference materials behind you, to offer you knowledge and support, and keep the area in front of you clear, so as to not clutter your views and so your thoughts.

Seating and relaxation furniture

○ If there is space, you may have a sofa bed or daybed for relaxing during the working day or for accommodating guests. Reserve the best command position for your desk, but ensure the sleeping or sitting furniture is not in a compromised position, such as pointing towards the door.

CHALLENGING ROOM SHAPES

Small workspace with a desk positioned with the door behind you

- If you have no choice but to have your back to the door, you might feel vulnerable or watched. Close the door when you're working.

- Alternatively, you may place a mirror on your desk so that you can see if someone is coming up to you from behind.

- If you are in a vulnerable position, a chair with a high back will help protect you – although it may make things worse if it makes you feel even more uncertain of what's happening behind you.

Small workspace with desk facing wall

- A workstation facing a wall will make you feel suppressed, so choose a larger, deeper desk to distance yourself from the wall as much as possible.

- Add life to your wall. Hang pictures, notice boards and other visual interest to draw your eye in. Good imagery or artwork tends to add depth.

Workspace with too many windows and doors

- Although you want a workspace with a window, too many openings can make it hard for you to concentrate. Ensure that your desk position is well covered at the back and that you are in a command position in the room.

- Where the room is small and the window and doors are aligned, one in front and one behind you, you have a difficult decision to make. On balance, it is better to face the wall than have your back to the door.

96

- Your work area should be its own space. Even in an open-plan room that has other functions, choose a secluded corner to make your workstation and position your furniture to suggest the separate functions.

Workspace with no windows

- Use an office with no windows only for short periods at a time — such as for an online meeting.

- Never spend extended periods of time in a space where you rely on artificial lighting, even during the daytime.

SHARING WORKSPACE

Command space

If everyone works as equals, plan the room so that nobody is in a compromised command position (see illustrations, page 98). If one person has a larger desk than another, the room will be unbalanced and that may lead to conflict. If there is a hierarchy, the most senior person should take the command position.

If you work in an office with one other person, position the desks so that it's not possible for you to look at each other's work. A good way to achieve this is to have two desks facing each other.

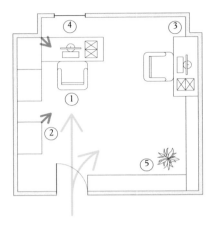

BAD

→ Chi flow and circulation

→ Aggressive, pointed elements

1 Seat is vulnerable, with back towards the door

2 Floating cabinets with sharp corners

3 Few windows providing limited light and air

4 Window in front of desk causes glare

5 Drying plant with no access to light shows decay

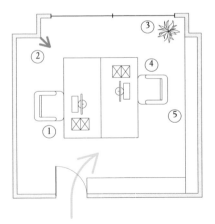

GOOD

→ Chi flow and circulation

→ Aggressive, pointed elements

1 Seat may not be in command position, but it's not vulnerable

2 Seats placed so that exposed corners do not point towards anyone

3 Large windows for ventilation with plants to signify growth

4 Seat in command position with soft light from the side

5 Solid wall of shelves to represent stability and knowledge

BEDROOM

The bedroom is a place of rest, a sanctuary from the outside world.
It is your place to recharge and forget about the tasks of everyday life.
The goal is to create a neutral, calming bedroom space, where you do
not think, and your mind lets go and relaxes.

LOCATION

Locate your bedroom far from the main entrance to your home, past the more public rooms (such as the living room and dining room). If your bedroom is close to the front door, keep the bedroom door shut and paint it a similar colour to the walls outside it, to make it more discreet. Ideally, your bedroom should not be too close to a bathroom, as sleeping is not associated with water or waste; and you should avoid a position close to a kitchen, because of the dominance of the fire element there.

FEELING AND PLAN

The bed is the main piece of furniture in this room. Place it symmetrically, with the rest of the space supporting its function – sleeping or resting. Ideally avoid having a desk, exercise area and TV in your bedroom. If that's unavoidable, at least allocate an area around the bed that is exclusively for rest.

- The main element of the bedroom is more earth than fire. While it may be a passionate room at times, the bedroom is mostly calming and restful. Play with horizontal lines and neutral, natural tones.

- Your bedroom should be square or rectangular and without sharp corners that point towards the bed. Avoid long rooms, which may form movement chi and make you feel like you are sleeping in a long corridor.

- A large bedroom can make us feel unprotected and lost. If your room is too big, create zones, with an area for sleeping and areas for sitting and relaxing, using rugs to anchor each zone. Try to protect the bed's immediate vicinity with sofas or benches, especially at its foot.

- While yang is a good thing for most rooms, bedrooms need a good amount of yin to give the feeling of restful calm. However, the room should never be too stale – it must always have a door and

100

a window to allow a healthy flow of chi. Never use a windowless room as a bedroom. As a rule of thumb, if a plant couldn't survive, the room is not suitable to sleep in.

○ If there are lots of windows in a bedroom, the vibrant energy of the sun and wind can too easily enter the room, disrupting sleep, and making you feel insecure and exposed. In this case, draw the curtains when sleeping.

○ If there is more than one door, the bedroom becomes a transitional space. Doors other than the entrance to your bedroom should lead to spaces exclusively for your use. For example, it's okay to have a door leading to a private balcony, but not okay to have one leading to a communal terrace.

○ Avoid keeping items such as televisions and computers, and even smartphones in the bedroom. Choose analogue gadgets over modern conveniences – for example, use a hot water bottle rather than an electric blanket.

○ Other items that bring yang energy to a room are aquariums, plants and images of dragons. Avoid having these in your bedroom. Although, of course, this rule is flexible. If any yang items give you a sense of calm or belonging, or if you regard your plants as your friends to share the space, they are okay.

THE AESTHETICS OF YOUR BED

Bed design

○ Choose a bed with a bedhead that is solid or padded, and the bigger and wider, the better. Avoid bare frames.

○ Choose a stable, not flimsy frame. Avoid water beds at all costs.

○ Four-poster beds can look severe. Low beds are more calm.

- Ensure the bed is raised off the floor to allow air to circulate around it. Storage beds are fine, but do not over-stuff the storage under the bed, as moisture will build up.

Dressing your bed

- Choose light, calm colours for your bedding. If you prefer dark, don't go for black.

- Make your bed when you get up to avoid any build-up of stale chi and prepare you for a peaceful return at the end of the day.

POSITIONING YOUR BED

Command position

The bed is for sleeping, and is the most important element in the room. It takes the command position.

- Place your bed with a solid wall behind it. Don't float it in the middle of the room or against a low partition.

- Avoid having your bedhead against a window. However, if you can't avoid that, have a strong bedhead or heavy curtains and ensure that the windowsill is at least higher than the bedhead.

- Avoid positioning your bed against any columns or against uneven or angled walls.

As well as benefiting from the stable tortoise position, your bed should, like the bird, have a space in front, so you don't feel cramped. It should have a broad, commanding view of the room, with a view of the main door, so you can see if anyone comes in. Inevitably, this means you should avoid placing your bed on the same wall as the main door, and avoid having furniture between the bed and door which might obscure this view. Too much space in front of your bed,

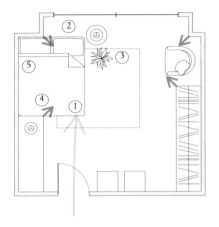

→ Chi flow and circulation

⇒ Aggressive, pointed elements

1 Chi flows directly to the foot of the bed
2 Bed lacks solid backing and is exposed
3 Plants (which signify energy) too close to the bed
4 Pointed furniture corners against the bed
5 Side of the bed pushed against a wall

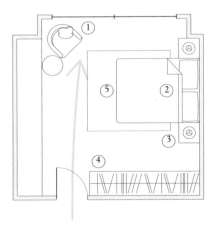

GOOD

→ Chi flow and circulation

⇒ Aggressive, pointed elements

1 Armchair diverts flow of chi
2 Bed head is against a solid wall and the bed is in the command position
3 Balanced arrangement with low-level bedside tables on either side
4 Full-width wardrobes with no exposed corners
5 Bed placed centrally anchors the room

however, creates too much chi. In short, aim for a balanced position for your bed.

○ Ensure that you can enter the bed from both sides, especially if there are two people sharing it. If you are single, this suggests that you are open to another person joining you.

○ Place a pair of matching bedside tables and lamps either side. They don't need to be identical, just have equal visual weight.

If you have trouble placing your bed in the classic command position, place it so that you are out of view from the room door to create a private space within the bedroom.

If the room is very small, or you prefer to allocate more space to other functions such as workspaces, you might have to place the bed towards the corner of the room with its side against a wall. This layout is not wrong and the bed is protected on all sides except one. But, the bed can serve only one person, and is best for happily single or very young people who are not yet ready for love or romance. If you do want romance in your life, avoid this placement.

Your bed and chi

It's important to avoid aggressive chi as much as possible in the bedroom. A classic rule of feng shui is: do not point your feet directly towards the main door to a room. This would direct chi straight up to you, but it also recalls the position of a coffin, or even of a breech birth, which is highly inauspicious. If your bed is directed towards the door, do not place it in line with the door.

○ If you can't put your bed elsewhere, place a screen to block the view of the door, or a heavy piece of furniture at the bed's foot.

○ If you have no choice and your bed points towards the door, look outside the room, and ensure that the space is not too busy or public.

Apart from your feet facing the door, it's not ideal to have your feet facing a window, as this generates too much movement chi. However, if the windows are not too big, or if your view is calming, it's okay.

- Ideally do not point your feet towards any other opening in the room. If you have a closet with a door, try to make the doors more discreet, and keep them closed.

- Even if the main door is not at your feet, keep it as far from the bed as possible.

- Mirrors behave like doors, so avoid having mirrors in the bedroom. If you have mirrors, it's best to place them so that you can't see your reflection from the bed.

Finally, avoid situations that create oppressive chi in your bedroom. This chi comes from physical objects that may be sharp or heavy.

Beams Avoid placing your bed under any overhead beams or structures as these represent blades looming over you. If there are beams, place the bed so that none is actually cutting across the bed. Try to cover beams with a false ceiling, or simply paint the beams the same colour as the rest of the ceiling.

Sloped ceilings If you live in an attic room, try to place your bed at the higher end of the ceiling and place it in a way that it is balanced – not having one side on a lower end than the other. If, though, your head will be on the lowest side of the ceiling, make sure you have a strong bedhead, and lights to lift that area. If you have a gabled roof, place your bed under the middle of the pitch.

Chandeliers Avoid heavy lights, fans or hanging sculptures over your bed. A light paper pendant, though, will work.

<u>Art</u> Never place heavy pictures or artwork over the bed, especially framed glass pictures, which are dangerous should they fall on you. It's fine to hang a light tapestry on the wall or to have a mural.

<u>Shelves</u> Never install shelves or any other type of wall furniture over your bed head.

OTHER POSITIONAL CONSIDERATIONS

Sleeping north

Some cultures discourage sleeping with your head pointing towards the north, as it is believed that the magnetic fields will interfere with your body. While it is true there are magnetic fields, they will not affect you so much, and the environment present around you is more important. There's no harm in following this principle in your bedroom, but don't let it compromise other considerations.

Outside wall

If you live in an older building, avoid placing your bed against an outside wall, because this will make you susceptible to outside temperature changes. However, in newer buildings, the influence of external temperature is no longer an issue.

OTHER FURNITURE

Walk-in wardrobes

These are desirable, but may pose problems if they aren't well positioned. The additional door leading to a wardrobe suggests that the sleeping area is a transitional room. Remember how, when you were young, the idea that something was lurking behind the wardrobe doors seemed scary? You want to avoid that energy, if possible. Try

106

to locate walk-in wardrobes outside of your sleeping area. If you can't avoid having them near where you sleep, and your wardrobe is located in your bedroom, make the door as discreet as possible.

Wardrobes (fitted and freestanding)

Fitted wardrobes allow more storage, look minimal and can disappear from view, which is preferable to freestanding and walk-in wardrobes. Similarly, a single, large unit is better than multiple smaller units, which create multiple sharp corners. If you do have freestanding wardrobes, use them as an opportunity to flatten out irregular walls.

Keep it tidy

Always keep wardrobes tidy to reflect your inner wellbeing and make it easier for you to find the clothes that you need when you need them.

Study and work tables (see page 127)

○ If you have to work in your bedroom, keep it to a minimum.

○ Do not sit on the bed while working. Aways have a dedicated chair where you sit.

○ Whether you have a desktop or a laptop, turn your computer off at night.

Note from Cliff If you're looking for love, a cramped, stuffed wardrobe signifies that there is no space for someone to join you in your life. Minimise your belongings to keep your wardrobes more spacious and help you feel less stifled.

Dressing tables

○ We use dressing tables for calmly getting ready, so these are more welcome in the bedroom than study tables.

○ If you have a mirror on your dressing table, try to point it away from the bed.

Side tables

○ Avoid sharp corners that will be close to your head while sleeping. Choose round side tables, or ensure the tables stand lower than the level of the mattress.

○ Use sturdy, enclosed side tables for both storage and the sense of stability that they give.

○ Avoid glass side tables. Glass is an energetic, cold material, much like a mirror.

○ Ensure that side tables are not too tall, and they don't loom over your head while you're sleeping.

ENSUITES AND ATTACHED BATHROOMS

With its association with water and waste, the bathroom is best located away from the sleeping area. Ideally, situate a private bathroom outside of your bedroom. If that's not possible, close the bathroom door while you sleep.

If you have an ensuite, or a bathroom near your bedroom, look at the position of the toilet. Avoid having the WC (toilet) share the same wall as the bed area. If you have a bathroom above your bedroom, ensure that the bedroom, and especially the location of the bed head, is not directly beneath the bath or WC. Apart from the negative energies this would create, it also has health considerations – if the building is not well insulated, water from a leaky bath or WC might mean you inhale mould while you sleep.

CHALLENGING ROOM SHAPES

Small bedrooms

If you have a small bedroom, planning its layout is like playing Tetris! The most important things to consider are function and flow.

- Start with the biggest pieces, and try to place them in the furthest corners of the room.

- Ensure that the bed is not cramped; keep it clear and easy to enter.

- Use a large, horizontal headboard that, if possible, extends the length of the wall it's on, to give the bed a commanding scale and make the room feel bigger.

Long rooms

- Place furniture horizontally instead of lengthways, including the bed, which should be perpendicular to the room. Be aware of the chi running along the room's length. Avoid placing your bed unprotected, without any furniture in front of it, at the end – the effects of which are similar to having a bed that faces a door.

- Hang artwork on the long walls to add width to the space, but don't use mirrors.

Irregular rooms

- Install built-in cabinets to square off a room.

- If you have an L-shaped room, try to square it off by giving the extra corner a different function, such as making it a wardrobe area.

- If you have a square room, the typical feng shui cure is to use mirrors to complete it. However, in the bedroom mirrors disrupt the sense of calm. Place artwork there to expand the view instead.

Rooms with too many windows and doors

○ Plot out where the walls are and where the doors and windows are, then identify how chi flows around the room.

○ Place the bed in a position that is away from these flows – in other words, in the calmest, darkest point of the room. If there isn't one, have heavy curtains to close off your windows at night.

○ Keep the internal doors in your bedroom closed, and make any unimportant doors discreet. For example, paint closet doors the same colour as the walls.

○ Darker colours make a room feel more intimate and cosy.

OTHER BEDROOMS

The principles for a shared bedroom or shared child's bedroom are mostly the same as the main bedroom, with some exceptions.

Shared bedrooms

○ The beds in a shared bedroom should be the same size to avoid signifying an imbalance between occupants, and they should have a space between them. Do not have another person's feet facing your head.

○ Avoid bunk beds, but if they are necessary, the older person should sleep in the top bunk.

○ Couples should sleep together. If you prefer to sleep separately, have two completely separate beds with a gap between. Do not have two single beds pushed together, which signifies a hidden and inescapable split between you.

○ Couples should not share rooms with a single, who represents a third party in the relationship.

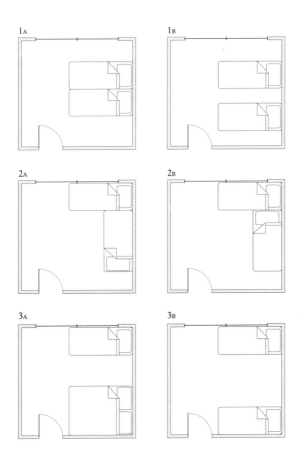

BAD	GOOD

1A Do not join two single beds together

1B It is better to split single beds apart

2A Do not point one's feet to another's head

2B Two bed heads against each other is acceptable

3A Avoid beds of different sizes

3B Both singles are better even if there's more space

- If possible, have a dedicated space for each person in the room. Try to organise the space so that nobody has to walk through the space of another to get to their own space.

A child's room

Children generally have different needs and energy levels to the adults in the household, so there are more differences in the feng shui of their bedrooms. Generally, the room is more energetic and less romantic, so there will be more yang.

- It is actually good for this room to have plants and computers, as children do not have the same need as adults for recuperation.

- Ideally, position a child's bedroom on the east side of the building in a room with windows that side, as this is where the sun rises and the energy is positive and represents growth.

- It may be tempting to place a child's desk so you can see the screen to check what they're doing, but avoid this to give your child more security and respect.

- Avoid open shelves for books, as these have the same effect as beams, cutting into you.

- Place a single bed with a long side against a wall to give the child more stability while sleeping.

Guest bedrooms

Treat guest bedrooms as you would any other bedroom. If the room has another function when you don't have guests and you have a temporary daybed or sofa bed, make sure it opens up to give the sleeping area the command position.

Temporary accommodation

○ Hotel rooms may be more invigorating for romantic situations, so mirrors or unconventional beds are fine here. However, remember this is a hotel room, and do not try to emulate any of these features in your own bedroom at home.

○ If you're sleeping in a dormitory or hostel, try to get the command position bed, at the far end of the room, as this will afford you more privacy.

○ On a cruise ship, choose a room with a window. Inside rooms have negative, stagnant chi.

○ If you're sleeping in a tent, follow the same principles as for a bedroom – in particular, do not face your feet towards the entrance of the tent.

BATHROOM

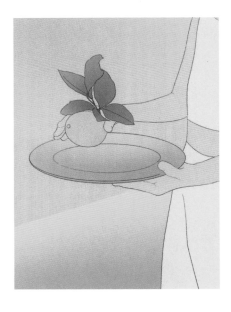

In China, bathrooms were traditionally located outside the main building of a home — they were undesirable places intended solely for the elimination of waste. This is why feng shui rarely refers to the bathroom in its principles. However, the improved smell and moisture control of the modern bathroom makes it a more acceptable room in feng shui terms. Furthermore, our lifestyles have changed. Far from being a place merely of waste disposal, a bathroom is now often regarded as a place to rejuvenate and achieve a sense of peace. As you take on the advice of this chapter, adapt its suggestions according to your own needs, wants and feelings for your bathroom space.

LOCATION

If you think of the home as the human body, the WC is basically the bottom, and functions as so. For this reason, position your bathroom as far from the other rooms of the house as possible. The general rule is that your bathroom should not be too prominent, nor on the main sightlines in the home. As long as you don't see it, the effects of its presence are mitigated.

○ Keeping the idea of the home as a body, never locate your bathroom near the mouth, which is the main door.

○ As the bathroom is associated with water, avoid placing it too close to the kitchen, say, which is linked with fire. Locate it away from the bedrooms.

○ Reserve the centre (or heart) of your home for more significant, functional spaces, such as the dining or living room, and avoid placing your bathroom here. If you have to, conceal the bathroom door and create focus on the more important rooms around it.

○ Never place the bathrooom, or worse, the WC within sight of the main door.

FEELING AND PLAN

Modern bathrooms can be places of calm, especially considered in the light of the ritual of bathing. Design the bathroom to reflect this ambiance. As the bathroom relates to the water element, avoid decorating yours in colours that destroy water, specifically fire colours, such as red. Features that evoke the elements of earth and wood balance the water nicely.

Note from Cliff In this section, we will call this room a bathroom instead of a toilet, and assume that there is a bathtub or shower in the room. As for the flush toilet that you sit on, we will call it a WC, which stands for water closet.

- Make sure your bathroom has good ventilation and air circulation to clear the moisture.

- Avoid positioning any mirrors to reflect the WC, and make sure you can't see the WC from the door.

- Natural light, or even direct sunshine, is best for a bathroom, but if that's not possible, use lighter colours for the walls and install bright lights.

- Always close the WC cover as the bowl is where we discharge waste, which left open could (according to some) accidentally flush away your fortunes.

- Plants bring an upward-growing chi, making them a good addition to a bathroom, but ensure they will survive. Generally, if you have sunlight (especially morning light), the humidity in the bathroom makes it an ideal place for plants to thrive.

- Try to make sure your bathroom has good natural ventilation. If that's not possible, install a good mechanical ventilator.

WC

Command position

Even though feng shui stigmatises it, the WC should take the command position in the room, as it's where you assume a sitting position and is a place where you spend time.

You shouldn't be able to see the WC from the doorway, and it shouldn't line up with the door at all – not only does it look bad, but you'll feel insecure if someone were to accidentally barge in. Following the classic command-position rule, the WC should be against a wall. This is also for practical reasons, as then you can locate the cisterns and waste pipes behind it. Do not place the WC against a window, or have it floating in the middle of the room.

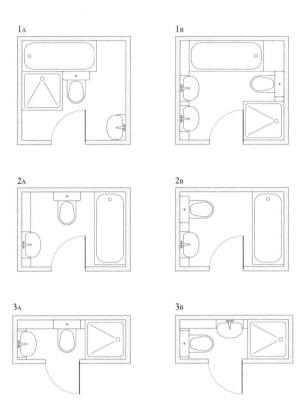

BAD	GOOD
1A Avoid floating fixtures	1B The bath is in the most prominent position
2A Avoid having the WC in line with the door	2B No fixtures are in line with the door
3A In small spaces, avoid placing the WC against the door	3B The WC is hidden in a more discreet area

- Place your WC away from your bathtub. Imagine yourself lying in the bath with the WC next to your face! A shower next to a WC is more acceptable, as showers tend to be within an enclosure.

- Ideally, a WC should have its own room within the bathroom, and if not, its own section.

- While the WC should not be in line with the door, like the command position of the bed, it should have sight of the door – for a sense of security.

BATHTUB AND SHOWER

Second in command

The bath and shower are also command elements in the room. While the WC is seen as the main element functionally, the bath or shower anchor the room visually, and remind us that the bathroom is also a place of peace and rejuvenation.

- Position your bath away from the WC.

- As with any classic command position, do not place the bath so that its feet line up with the door.

- You can locate a shower anywhere as this is an enclosed element and used for only short periods. Ideally, though, it should not be in line with the main door to the bathroom.

- Position your bath so that it's the first and most prominent feature in the room as you enter.

118

SINK AND VANITY CABINET

Third in command

Even though you might not spend that much time using them, the sink and vanity cabinet are important features of a bathroom. Try to place the sink with command principles in mind, so that your back is not facing the door while using it. The sink is also a useful tool for separating the WC and bathtub. Generally, place the vanity cabinet and mirror at right angles to the door.

CHALLENGING ROOM SHAPES

Small bathrooms

A bathroom is meant to be small, so size is less of an issue here – although it still needs to have all the equipment for its functions.

○ Plan the space to avoid needing to squeeze past anything to access the utilities.

○ A good trick is to share the standing space. The space in front of a WC, the space where you stand in front of a vanity unit and the space leading to the shower can all be the same space.

○ You may place fittings diagonally on corners if it helps to maximise space.

Windowless bathrooms

The most important thing is to prevent the air from becoming stale.

○ Install ventilators and vents.

○ Make the space as bright as you can, with lighting on the walls next to the mirrors as a priority. Avoid top-down lighting as this is harsh and not very flattering.

- As there are no windows, do not have plants in this room; they will die.

- Decorate the bathroom with mirrors and with luxury toiletries in your favourite scents.

- Use tiles made of natural stone, such as marble, to bring in nature.

- Large mirrors will expand the space inside a small bathroom and give the effect of windows.

Large bathrooms

Bathrooms are meant to be small, so a large bathroom presents a challenge. The best solution is to design a room that focuses on relaxation, rather than utility.

- Anchor the bathroom on the bathtub.

- Enclose the WC in its own space, or hide it from view in some other way.

- Add a separate shower area that is generous and easy to enter.

Irregular bathrooms

- Bathrooms work well in irregular-shaped spaces as they have a variety of functions.

- If you have any awkward corners, take advantage of them by placing the WC in one of them to form a private pocket of space.

- Place built-in cabinets for essential storage in any niches.

- Make custom, tiled shower enclosures within awkward shapes.

120

SHARED
SPACES

Not everyone has the luxury of having separate rooms for every purpose – or even wants that! Perhaps you have a modern, open-plan living area, or you are renting a room in a shared house or dorm, or your entire home fits within a single studio space. If you have pets, you'll need to incorporate their specific needs into your space as well.

The general rule is that any shared space should be sectioned into its different uses. A shared space should only appear shared – the various functions will always have their own sections. It's never a good idea to mix up these sections too much (that is, sitting on your bed to work, or sitting on your sofa to have dinner). Even transformable furniture (such as fold-down beds or dining tables) should be kept to a minimum. Having a designated place for the various types of activity aligns with our natural tendency to make mental connections to place. It's the same principle that tells us it's better to place a cat's food bowl and water bowl in separate places, because hunting and finding water are different feline activities. In feng shui, the goal is always to match our spaces to our natural tendencies as much as possible.

The main way to section out your space is by activity level. There are two main requirements that affect most people:

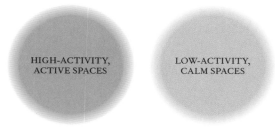

HIGH-ACTIVITY, ACTIVE SPACES

LOW-ACTIVITY, CALM SPACES

Depending on how you use your space, you might need to section it further:

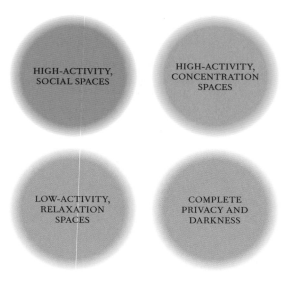

HIGH-ACTIVITY, SOCIAL SPACES

HIGH-ACTIVITY, CONCENTRATION SPACES

LOW-ACTIVITY, RELAXATION SPACES

COMPLETE PRIVACY AND DARKNESS

Once you've marked out your spaces, acknowledge their different physical qualities and arrange those activities that are similar and require similar energy levels in spaces that are close to each other. It's important to consider activity level rather than room type, because, for example, a living space for one person may be calm and private (so a good place to consider situating a bed next to), while for another person it might be a social space.

The rule is always the same: determine the activity levels and needs of each function and allocate the sector that best matches those criteria.

LIVING AND DINING

Living and dining areas are often combined in open-plan living. These two are very similar in terms of energy level, so follow the same rules as you would for a standard living or dining room, with the following in mind:

○ Do not let the dining table encroach into the living space.

○ Place a low console or other dividing furniture piece to separate the zones.

○ Place the dining area on the side closer to the kitchen. Or, if the kitchen is elsewhere in the house, keep the dining area closer to the entrance of the room and at the more active end of the room, closer to the main circulation paths or windows. (This is because the living area is slightly calmer in comparison.)

○ Decorate the areas as you would a separate dining or living room. If you want to have pendant lamps, hang them only over the dining area, or have the same in both areas.

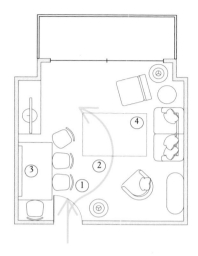

BAD

→ Chi flow and circulation

1 No proper entry area
2 Living and dining areas are not defined
3 Dining area feels cramped and tight
4 Seating arranged to focus towards the wall

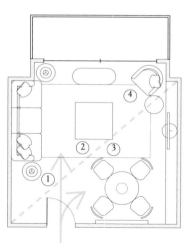

GOOD

→ Chi flow and circulation

1 Clear space to pause before entering
2 Defined living and dining spaces either side of an imaginary diagonal line
3 Each area feels spacious yet separate
4 Seating arranged to create focus within the living area

LIVING, DINING AND KITCHEN

Things become slightly more complex when you combine the living room, dining room and kitchen. Traditionally, the kitchen is a service area to be hidden, while the dining room is a central place to be celebrated. In this situation, see the kitchen as an attachment to the living and dining areas, which guide the feeling of the space. Follow the rules as for a combined living and dining room, then:

○ Make the kitchen as calm as possible. Use low cabinets and neutral colours. Don't hide the kitchen, but respect the calm side of the home.

○ Keep the kitchen tidy at all times, store appliances away, and keep worktop appliances to a minimum. On balance, it's more important to divide the dining room from the living room, than the dining room from the kitchen.

○ If you have a sit-up kitchen counter, face the seats towards the kitchen and ensure the dining table can seat more than the counter.

○ Hang mirrors to reflect only the dining side, and not the kitchen. When in doubt, avoid mirrors altogether.

○ Hang a pendant light over the dining table to bring more weight to the table area, but do not hang anything prominent over the kitchen counter, as the two will compete.

○ If there is no space for a dining table, remove the sit-up counter and have a dining table instead, as this is an important part of a sense of place and family.

DINING ROOM AND KITCHEN

If the kitchen is big enough to contain your dining table, this becomes a mixed space. In general, follow the rules for the kitchen, but here are some additional simple guidelines to follow for the table:

- Avoid upholstered seats or cushions, minimising the plush elements of a room.

- Keep the dining area casual-looking – if it's too formal it will clash with the feel of the kitchen.

- Even though in this scenario the kitchen plays the more prominent role, pendant lights should always focus over the dining table.

- If you eat only at the kitchen counter and don't have a dining table, keep the counter clear and decorate it as you would a table. Designate a specific area of the counter specifically for kitchen activities, such as preparing and cooking food, and decorate the counter with something pleasing, such as a bowl of fruit.

WORKING IN THE LIVING SPACE OR KITCHEN

It's increasingly common to work in the living areas, and especially on the dining table or at the kitchen counter. If you can, though, it's far better to have a designated work space, and you should certainly avoid working at the kitchen counter. Try to set up a proper desk on the side of your living area, even if it is a small one.

- Where you have space for a desk, place it as far from the kitchen as possible, away from circulation areas and, if possible, away from the entrance to the room.

- If you need to work on the dining table, keep a section of it for work and avoid moving your things back and forth when it's time to eat (if the table is large enough). If you work on a smaller dining table, think of the table as your office and treat the dining function as a temporary event, rather than the other way round.

- Remove fruits and flowers when you're working. When you're done, place them back on to the table.

- Keep study materials and books away. If it is a permanent arrangement and you have lots of books for your work, it's better to have the desk and shelves closer to the living area.

- Keep the TV switched off when you work.

- Do not work while other people are cooking, as this creates a clash of activity levels and you'll find it difficult to concentrate.

BEDROOM AND STUDY

Possibly the most common shared space is that of the bedroom and study – think students in dorms, those staying in hotel rooms, or almost any home where there is no designated workspace. As a rule of thumb, it's better to work in the dining or living areas than in a bedroom, if possible. If you have to work in your bedroom:

- Separate the sleeping and working areas, and make them as defined as possible, following the rules for an office for the study area (see pages 90–98) and the rules for a bedroom for the sleeping area (see pages 99–113).

- Try to keep the study area closer to the door, and the sleeping area at the rear of the room.

- Keep the study area in the more yang part of the room, where there is more light from the windows. You might face a dilemma here, as the rear of the room is where the windows often are, and this contradicts the previous advice to keep the bed further from the door. In this case, make a decision based on your natural tendencies. For example, if you really need natural light to work, place the desk on the window side, or if you feel too vulnerable sleeping close to the door, place the bed there instead.

- If the bed is very close to the door, place it in a protected position in a niche.

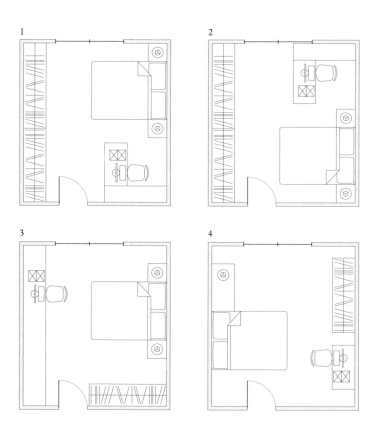

1   If the sleeping position is important, place the bed in the command position; however, the desk might be dark

2   If work is important, place the desk close to the window with more light, but the bed might be closer to the door than is ideal

3   A compromise: both the bed and the desk are at the end of the room

4   Avoid placing both the bed and the desk too close to the room's entrance

BEDROOM AND OTHER FUNCTIONS

Exercise, entertainment and socialising, and myriad other activities often take place in a bedroom – especially if you share a house. The main thing to remember is that the bed is reserved for rest, so mark an area around the bed and keep it calm. Then, plan your functions according to activity level: locate the highest activity functions further from the bed, and the most relaxing ones closer to the bed.

STUDIO APARTMENTS

Even if your entire home is in a single space, try to have a separate kitchen as it's very important that the kitchen and the sleeping areas do not clash. It's okay if the living area is shared with the bedroom, but not the dining area and especially not the kitchen. If your space is completely open, layer the functions:

Bed area This will be the most private part of the space, usually at the end of the room or at the rear of the space.

Living area This will follow the bed area, and act as a buffer between the dining and kitchen areas and the sleeping area.

Dining area Situate this next to the living area. In smaller studio spaces, you could remove the dining table entirely and use the counter. Note that wherever everything else is, it is important for the dining table to be close to the kitchen. This rule may override others.

Kitchen Keep this as far from the sleeping area as possible, preferably towards the windows.

Entrance Arrange furniture to create an entry area around the door, but avoid placing it directly at the entrance or blocking the way.

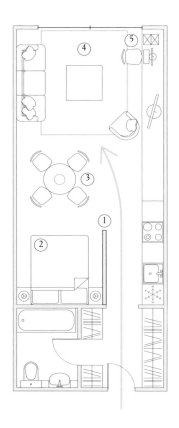

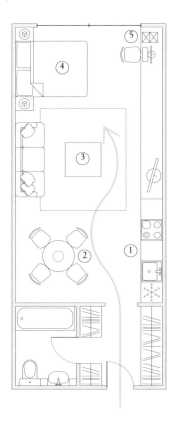

STUDIO OPTION 1

→ Chi flow and circulation

1   Divider between the kitchen and bedroom
2   Bed is in quietest part of the room
3   Dining area is close to the kitchen
4   Living area is in the brightest part
    of the room
5   Study area enjoys natural light

STUDIO OPTION 2

→ Chi flow and circulation

1   Kitchen feels spacious next to the
    dining area
2   Dining table is closest to the kitchen
3   Living area is in the darker part of the room
4   Bedroom is in the furthest but brightest
    section of the room
5   Study area enjoys natural light

<u>Bathroom</u> Often the bathroom is in the quietest and darkest part of the room, which coincides with where the sleeping area should be. This is fine, as long as you close the door.

KEEPING PETS

If you're sharing your space with animal friends, remember they have feelings, too. In fact, animals may feel the effects of feng shui and placement more than we do.

Animals want to be able to see what's going on in the room and, uncontained, will naturally find their command position. If you have a puppy that is crated, place the crate so that the puppy can see who is coming through the door. Hearing noises without being able to identify the cause of them causes anxiety. If you have a cat 'tree', place it so that when the cat is perched, it is close to you and can also see the room. If you don't have a cat tree, give your cat another high-up place where they can perch.

Keep birds, rodents, fish and reptiles (contained in a cage or tank) away from the kitchen (which may emit fumes that are toxic to these animals) or bathroom (which can be too humid). Keep them in more pleasant areas, such as the living room, but avoid the bedroom as they give off too much energy at night to allow for restful human sleep. Place a bird cage against a wall, rather than in the middle of the room, to give your bird a sense of protection, and away from an entrance, which has too much going on.

<u>Eating and toileting</u> Keep food and waste areas away from each other (for a cat's litter tray, try to create a private space) and your pets' sleeping area. Ideally, locate food bowls close to where you eat.

Styling

5

A lot of feng shui is about feeling good about a home –
and you will feel good when things look nice. The next step,
then, is to turn your house into a home. Even if you have
a functional home that works well, and have all the furniture
in the right places, your spaces can lack soul and life. In feng
shui, styling, colour and light bring the five elements, as well
as the balance of yin and yang into a space. While applying
personality to your home is fun, it is also one of the most
difficult things to get right – this chapter is here to help.

IMPRESSIONS

You have only one chance to make a first impression. This is not just for your guests or people coming to your home for the first time. The most important person that you need to impress is yourself!

Think about this: every time you come home after a long day at work or after a long holiday, what do you feel when you look into your hallway? Do you feel disappointed, frustrated, stifled? Or do you feel welcome, calm and glad to be home?

THE FIRST VIEW

You don't need to feel overwhelmed when designing a space, as long as you know this secret: all you need to do is design it so that it looks good from one angle. This is the direction that you approach it – usually the entrance to the room.

By doing this you have set the impression of the home, so even if the other angles don't look as good, you've made the powerful initial impression. This is how you do it.

<u>Find the spots</u> Take a plan of your home and draw a walking path from the main entrance to each room in the house. You can make multiple paths but they must always be in only one direction. At the entrance to every notable space, mark a spot. This is the spot from where that room should look good.

<u>Pick the key item</u> From the viewpoint you have marked, the key item in the room should anchor your view. This is usually the sofa, desk, dining table or bed, depending on the room. Of course, the actual positioning of the furniture should still depend on the feng shui layouts and command positions, but you can adjust the visual weight so that this anchor piece will stand out. This is important because the key item symbolises the function of the room. By making this item visually prominent, you know exactly what the room is intended for as soon as you enter.

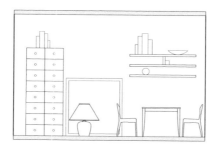

BAD

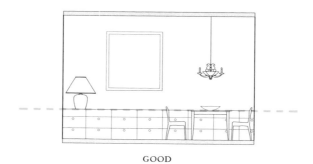

GOOD

- - - - - - Above this line, keep the room clean and free from clutter

<u>Compose the image</u> Now, start to compose your view. The way you design this view should align with the feeling of the space. For example, a living room should feel grand and symmetrical, with comfortable seats clearly visible to make it appear more inviting. A bedroom should instantly feel calm and soothing, with the bed taking centre stage with lots of horizontal, calming lines and subtle lighting.

<u>Divide your room</u> To make a space feel considered and beautiful, divide your room into a top and bottom section. The lower section – below an imaginary line drawn one-third of the way up the wall from the floor – is where you keep all storage furniture or utilitarian things. Avoid high bookshelves or wall-mounted shelves here, or stacking boxes high up. The top two-thirds of your room should be empty, reserved only for decorative items, such as pictures, lamps, plants or ornaments. A good way to define this line is to find the height of your main piece of furniture – be it a console or a kitchen counter, say – and use this as the imaginary dividing height.

CLUTTER AND STORAGE

In every home, there is stuff. When this stuff loses its focus and starts to take over the space, it becomes clutter. While some people say that they find comfort in clutter, this is true only if there is method – in which case this is no longer clutter! Clutter is when things are strewn around in an uncontrolled fashion against our will. In feng shui terms, this is bad. Instead, spaces need to flow freely with our mind.

CATEGORISE EVERYTHING

Clearing clutter is not just hiding everything from view. Your life is a huge archive, and you need to store it with an archivist's rigour. Before even picking up the first item from the floor, start to devise a system. Categorise storage locations in a logical way. Have a space for clean clothes, dirty clothes, a place for books and stationery.

Within each category, categorise once more; so within the place for stationery, have a box for pens, another for scissors and another for sharpeners. Avoid 'miscellaneous' boxes and always find a category for everything. When devising your own system, remember that every item has symbolism, and needs to be in the right section of your home. For example, keep books and stationery where you use them most (such as in the study), or toiletries near the bathroom. Over the page is a sample list.

Storage plan

- *Study* – books, stationery
- *Bedroom* – clothes
- *Bathroom* – toiletries and first aid
- *Store room* – tools, cleaning items
- *Kitchen* – cooking things
- *Dining room* – cutlery and crockery
- *Living room* – curiosities and objects for display

Once you've allocated everything to a category, sorting is going to be easy. Start to move all your things to the relevant area – and I do mean everything. (Incidentally, if you have cookbooks, they belong on the bookshelf, not in the kitchen.) Slowly but surely, you will not only declutter your home, but your mind as well.

Think of your home as a map: if you're going to get lost in it, you'll never feel like you belong. Once you have your own system for navigating the paths and spaces on the map, you just need to remember the logic to find something – instantly, without needing to remember where you put it. In fact, a successful storage solution means that even a stranger would be able to locate things intuitively. Think of it like this: when you visit someone else's kitchen, you will likely know instinctively where they keep their cutlery. If you need a reminder of where your things are, opt for labels on doors (avoid clear glass doors, as the messy insides will be visible).

Even if your storage areas are hidden from view, always keep them organised. Not just to help you locate things: they represent your past and symbolise the room you have for your future.

PLACEMENT OF THINGS

After you have cleared your clutter, look at the arrangement of your furnishings. Remember: too much furniture is considered clutter. Never block doorways as to do so indicates that you have a blocked approach to the world.

TASTE AND PREFERENCE

More than impressions and clutter, taste is about who you are, and *this* forms a personal link between you and your space. Have you ever been asked: 'Are you a morning lark or night owl?' This question goes deeper than just whether you prefer to get up early or stay up late. Being a lark or an owl is instinctive and natural – you don't choose it. Feng shui is similarly about crafting your environment to match your natural tendencies. In doing so, your home will become a place where you are most at ease and comfortable. But, how do you know what your tastes and preferences are?

Numerology Feng shui has long aimed to use numerology to predict our natural tendencies and choices. The processes are called the *ba zi* and the Four Pillars of Destiny, which are based on a person's specific numbers, such as their birth year, month, day and hour. This metaphysical approach aims to predict things such as which are your lucky directions or lucky year or decade cycles. There is a level of interpretation to the results, as well as the influence from external factors, such as where you were raised and your upbringing. Leave interpretation to the experts and accept their readings with caution.

Feel A much easier – and arguably more accurate – way to find your natural tendencies is simply to ask yourself what you like. Here's an exercise to help you identify your style and give you an idea of your sensitivities and preferences. Your choice of colours, textures and materials determines the type of element that appeals to you.

1   Find a pen and piece of paper. Pick a room in your home
    (it could be the room you're now sitting in) and look around.

2   Chances are that at some point you made a feng shui decision
    in this room even without knowing it, such as what pictures
    to hang, or the colour of the walls, or the style of the bedding.
    Pick out the things you love about the room and note them
    down in the order they occur to you.

3   Now pick out the things you hate, again noting them down
    in order. Maybe there are artefacts that you chose a long time
    ago that now make you cringe.

4   Look back over your lists. The things you noticed first are the
    things that affect you most. Quickly, remove all the things you
    hate from the space and look again. Now you will start to see
    a more coherent image of your tastes and preferences.

Passion Pick one item in your home that you absolutely love –
everyone has one! This might be something you chanced upon and
absolutely fell in love with, perhaps. You might even have spent time
saving up enough money to afford it. It could be a piece of décor
(a lamp or an artwork) or a piece of jewellery or a watch, or even
a piece of technology (a TV or set of headphones). You don't have
to care about the design or look of it, you just need to remember that
feeling of love. In everything that you buy, always remember this
feeling, and take a moment to make a thoughtful decision before you
actually pay for anything. Your taste may seem inconsistent at first,
but you will soon see a pattern that is then reflected in your home.

With this newfound self-knowledge from identifying how you
feel about items in your home, and finding a specific item you're
passionate about, you can make more thoughtful decisions when
styling your space.

ARTIFICIAL LIGHTING

Rooms that face different directions have different lighting needs. We have learned how natural lighting affects a room – but what happens at night? Artificial lighting can change and alter the sense of a space.

According to the principles of feng shui, supplementing any natural phenomenon (such as light) needs the utmost consideration. When designing the lighting scheme in a room, remember that you are designing with shadow as much as you are with light. The goal is not to light up a room as evenly or brightly as possible, but to thoughtfully choreograph the balance of yin and yang in a space.

TYPES OF LIGHT BULB

When it comes to artificial lighting, we need to start with the bulbs. How a light bulb feels depends on two things: the colour of the temperature and the diffusion of the emitted light. Colour temperature is the yellowness of a light and is determined by Kelvins, which is a number ranging from about 1500 to 6500 (see below). Whichever yellowness you choose, be sure that all the light bulbs in a room are the same.

<u>2700K</u> These aim to match the colour of natural tungsten filaments, which are actually 3000K. However, in LED bulbs, the colours are more red and less natural, so it's better to choose something around 2700K–2900K to match (each brand will vary). Don't go warmer than 2500K, or the light will look unnaturally orange.

<u>3500K</u> Think fluorescent studio lamps or office lighting.

<u>4000K and above</u> When the colour temperature mimics daylight, it becomes unnatural, and will confuse your senses. Use bulbs of 4000K or above only if your work requires it, or if you need to replace the energy of the sun during long winter months.

Note from Cliff For study rooms where light is important, consider using reflected light. An easy way to do this is to have a strong uplighter, and shine it against a white ceiling. This will give the room a washed-out, but soft glow, which will not cast any shadows.

DIFFUSION

The way the light diffuses into the room comes from the type
of light-bulb coating. If your light bulb is a frosted white sphere,
its light will be diffused and soft; if it's a clear glass bulb, the light
will be dazzling and piercing. Neither is better, but remember that
dazzling light is yang, while soft, diffused light is yin. Clear bulbs
will cast harder shadows and command more attention, while opaque
(sometimes called opal) bulbs will give a softer glow and recede
into the background.

CLEAR BULBS
HARD LIGHT

FROSTED BULBS
DIFFUSED LIGHT

HOW TO LIGHT A ROOM

Generally, it's better to use multiple light sources to light up a single
space, because in the natural environment, internal spaces receive
light from many different directions, from openings in the walls,
flames, or reflections from the ground. If we can mimic these natural
phenomena, our eyes feel more at ease. This is why for windowless
rooms, it's better to have soft light washed against walls rather than
a piercing central light source.

1   Plot out the areas with higher levels of activity, or areas that are
     the focus of a room, such as the dining area or a reading nook.
     Mark out the areas with the least amount of activity, or receding
     areas, such as unused corners, storage areas, or pathways.

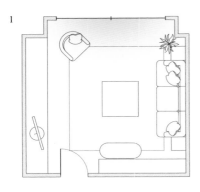

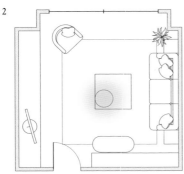

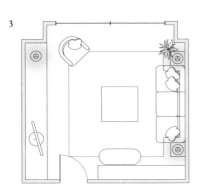

1   Position lights where light
    seems most natural – usually
    closer to the windows
2   Avoid a single point of light,
    which cause spaces to feel flat
    and dull
3   Aim for several points of low
    lighting, with more lighting
    closer to the windows; allow
    some corners to stay in shadow
    for depth and variation

2   Light the areas of higher activity and make the areas with lower activity darker – by mixing light and shadow you can create a more beautiful space.

3   The type of bulb you use will depend on the room and the feeling you want to achieve. For example, in yang rooms (such as the living or dining rooms), you may use clear bulbs, which give a more dazzling light. In bedrooms, always use softer diffused light from opaque (opal) bulbs. If in doubt, use the softer lights with shades.

Once you've got to grips with the principles of lighting a room, think about the different types of light source. It's good to have a mixture of these in every room, as each has its strong points.

FLOOR AND TABLE LAMPS

The staples of any lighting scheme, floor and table lamps represent the simplest forms of artificial lighting, harking back to candles and oil lamps, where light is from a lower, side source. Floor lights are useful to add height to low ceilings, or to bring down the scale of higher ceilings. Table lamps act as sculptural pieces to anchor consoles or side tables. The most common type of table or floor lamp is the conical lampshade, which references the fire element, an apt symbol for a light. These lamps make a room feel calm.

Ideally, you should place diffused floor and table lamps in corners, particularly ones where you want to increase the yang energy, remembering that the balance of yin is important in any space.

I would recommend lighting three out of four corners of a room according to the activity level in the room (see page 122), so that there are designated corners of yin and to create balance. You can also place lights at the end of corridors or long rooms to bring those spaces forward. Another tip is to locate lights in front of windows, because this is a natural place for a source of light.

Placed at the low ends of sloped ceilings or pitched roofs, table or floor lamps have the effect of 'lifting' oppressive, low ceilings. If you have a bed inside a niche, placing lights inside would also elevate the space. If your room is irregular, you can use floor or table lamps to light up darker corners to square off the room.

HANGING LIGHTS

Hanging lights provide a convenient, central source of light, reminding us of the sun and moon – the most natural sources of light of all. There are two main types:

Chandelier or lantern

A central hanging chandelier always grabs the most attention – even if you have a very expensive sofa or statement rug beneath it. This important piece determines the look and feel of a space.

Round shades are best, as they represent fullness and perfection; they reference metal and even symbolise heaven. Triangular shapes echo fire, which is linked to light, and form a potent symbol in the middle of the room. Do not hang square pendants or shades as they represent earth, which should be on the ground. This also goes for vertical rectangles or wavy shapes, as these are for water and wood, which should also be grounded. If choosing a pendant light in a fluid shape, make sure the fire and sparkle of the light overcomes the feeling of water.

Hang only one statement chandelier per space. If your ceiling is high enough, hang it in the middle of the room above everything else. If not, hang it over the dining table or a coffee table (if it's in the living room) so that it's not in the way.

If your room is very large and you really want to hang two pendants, try to make sure that the two of them match. If the room is small and has a low ceiling, but you still really wish to hang a pendant, I suggest hanging it near the corner over a side table. That way, it will behave like a floor lamp.

148

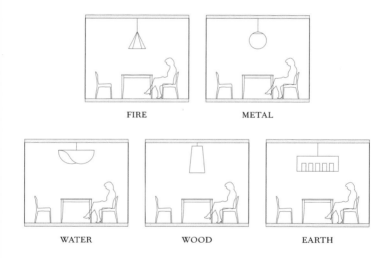

FIRE　　　　METAL

WATER　　　WOOD　　　EARTH

Downlight pendant

Downlight pendants are more functional than chandeliers, and exist to light a specific surface, like a table. For this reason, hang them only above dining areas, kitchens or study rooms, not in living rooms or entryways. Don't hang a downlight pendant any higher than your head – as a general rule, you should not be able to see the bulb inside it. It should also not be too big.

Pick triangles or cones as they represent fire, which gives light. Hemispheres are fine, too. As with the chandeliers, avoid squares and fluid shapes, as these represent earth and water, which should be on the ground.

Desk or other task lights

Libraries and workshops, where you need to direct light to be able to see closely for work or a particular activity, are the most common settings for 'task' lights. Place them only on work tables, side tables where you have a place to sit and read, or as floor lamps next to armchairs. Avoid using task lighting in your bedroom – a diffused table lamp is more suitable for the space.

UPLIGHTERS

Giving the visual effect of fire, uplighters are best in rooms with no windows or very low ceilings. They lead the eye downwards, and wash light against the walls mimicking the way light reflects off water in windowless caves and grottoes. Uplighters are also a good way to highlight architectural features in grander spaces.

CEILING AND WALL LIGHTS

Where there is no height for a pendant light, or no space for a floor or table light, try using ceiling and wall lights.

Track and spotlights

These do not have much of a presence, but offer directable light, which helps you to control the light and shadow, or yin and yang, of a space. When you have directable lights, focus them on objects around the room, such as artwork on the wall, or tables. Do not point them to random spots on the floor, or towards seating.

Recessed lighting

This is a clean way to bring light into a room, although you need to plan carefully the position of each light – people often make a light grid without thinking. When designing recessed lights, position them over where you want to create depth and shadow. Position lights over table tops and avoid putting them over seating areas. Leave shadows in unusable areas, such as passageways or corridors.

Mounted ceiling lights

These often elaborate designs are more like compressed chandeliers, and can look beautiful in the right settings. Try to avoid flush-mounted ceiling fixtures as they tend to produce flat and dull results. For surface-mounted lights, avoid squares, as they recall earth. The only suitable shape for surface-mounted ceiling lights is the circle, which recalls heaven.

Wall-mounted lights

Choose shapes that reflect light on to the wall. Make the wall lights as discreet as possible, unless they are statement wall pieces and are meant to behave like art (see pages 157–9).

COLOURS

Even though colour affects how you feel about each room in your home and changes the mood of a space (particularly whether the colour is light or dark), you don't need to be afraid of it. There are feng shui principles to learn when considering colour in your home, but all you really need to do is to think about it in the same way you think about colour in nature. The effects of colour in a space influence the balance of yin and yang.

There is a painting by J.M.W. Turner, titled *Helvoetsluys*, which is a seascape caught in transition, moments before a storm, with ships negotiating choppy waves. At the bottom of the painting, close to the edge, there is a small but striking rectangle of red paint. A red buoy, insignificant yet moving, stands out from the scene, and transforms it entirely. This painting exemplifies how balance in colour is not about having equal size or weight, but about having presence.

WHITE

First, let's talk about white. Don't assume that white should be
the default neutral colour. To choose to paint a room white is a very
conscious decision, because white is not a base colour. It represents
the metal element and sits at the end of the colour spectrum, leaving
very little room for interpretation. If you're unsure about white,
a far more neutral and versatile tone is a mid-grey.

COLOUR TEMPERATURE OF A SPACE

Before you choose a colour to paint your room, ask yourself: is this
room warm or cool? Think back to when we were describing the
direction of rooms, and what each means. For example, rooms that
face south–west (or north–west in the southern hemisphere) tend to
get more sunlight during the day and generally feel warmer, whereas
rooms facing away from the sun tend to feel cooler.

Whatever colours you choose for your rooms, keep their tones
consistent with one another. Even seemingly monochromatic tones
have warm and cool ranges.

SATURATION

The less saturated a colour, the calmer and more muted it feels. If you
feel unsure about what colour to paint your room, opt for shades with
lower saturation. Instead of yellow, go for tan or sand; and instead
of bright red, go for terracotta. Note that the saturation of a colour
can change the feng shui element it represents. A grey-blue would
represent water, while a very saturated blue is closer to wood.

THE ELEMENTS

We categorise colours through their elements, and the five elements are each represented by a colour range. Each range isn't just about hue, but also about the feeling it creates, which is a combination of the factors we encountered on the previous pages: light/dark, temperature and saturation.

<u>Fire</u> Representing energy and passion, fire is bright, saturated and vibrant, but you should use it sparingly in warm–hot shades of red and deep orange. If you do decide to paint an entire wall in reddish tones, desaturate it to bring it closer to terracotta and the earth element. Fire should burn vibrantly in small but powerful doses. Too much fire can disrupt sleep.

<u>Earth</u> Representing balance, calm and inner peace, earth should be neutral, subdued and natural. Yellows and natural, light browns represent the earth element, and these are suitable for large areas or entire walls. When choosing this element for larger areas, aim for less saturated tones, leaning more to warm greys than yellows. Somewhat famously, yellow is a colour that enhances your appetite.

Metal Representing precision, transformation and density, metal should be clean, bright and pristine, mostly white, but also lighter tones of blue and grey. When a shade of grey darkens past the midpoint, it becomes water (see below). White makes a nice accent tone against lighter grey backdrops. If you decide to use white for entire walls or rooms, remember that it is a strong colour in its own right (see page 153) and anticipate a slightly tense atmosphere in the room. Metal colours are good for a study area.

Water Representing fluidity and a downward search, water should be dark, mysterious, deep and cool, with blacks, deep blues and dark greys. When blues get too light, they become wood (see below). Never use pure black to paint a room. Instead, go for very dark tones of blue or brown – the very slight undertone of colour will allow the eye to rest. Pure black is strong – use it sparingly as accents or for framing. Blue suppresses the appetite, so avoid using it in the dining room.

Wood Representing growth, vitality and life, wood should be bright, and saturated in cool vibrant shades of mainly green (not brown!) and lighter shades of blue. When used with brown, wood should have greens to represent life. Showcase wood through plants and natural materials. If you're painting a wall green, opt for very subtle colours, such as a grey with slight green undertones.

ART AND SCULPTURE

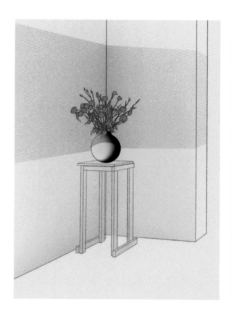

In every home there are objects and trinkets that define our interests and passions. For some people these are souvenirs from travel, for others they may be carefully chosen pieces or precious heirlooms. This chapter is not about telling you what you should get, but rather to help you understand the significance of the various shapes and forms of any artefacts so that you can get the right energy out of them (by putting them in a better space, perhaps). Remember that your belongings tell a personal story, so be proud of them.

156

WALL OBJECTS

Wall art is interesting because it doesn't take up any physical space, but it can have a big impact on a room. Let's start with two-dimensional artwork – photographs, framed prints or paintings, or even murals. If your wall has a feature colour or wallpaper, this is also a type of art in its own right.

Types of wall object

There is no right type of art – it can be anything from paintings to photographs, portraits to landscapes, religious imagery to graphic prints or posters. Size, colour, texture and, of course, image are all variable. What matters are the thoughts or memories that a wall object evokes, that you love it, that it was something you felt passionate about the moment you saw it, and that it is something that holds a special place in your heart.

There is, however, a very wrong type of wall art. Anything that you buy 'for the sake of' filling a wall is not good. If you don't feel anything for a piece of wall art, then it's not right. Commercially produced art, such as canvas prints or word art, are designed to appeal to as general a population as possible. Remember, you will look at these artworks every single day, and they will slowly but surely leave an impact on you. Choose only items have true meaning for you.

Work out where to display your art by matching its feel and tone to that of the space. Look at the contents of your image, and decide what kind of feelings it gives you. Where in your home do those feelings most belong?

Clocks Locate your clocks where you want to experience a sense of haste, precision and awareness – all characteristics of a clock. Also consider the design (the shape and colour, and the typography of the numbers). Avoid putting clocks in the dining room and bedroom, where no one wants to feel under time pressure.

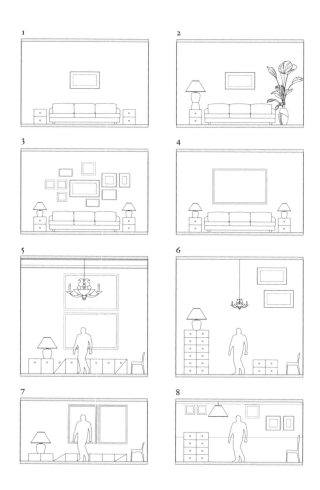

1   Avoid hanging artwork that is too small
2   Balance small artwork with tall elements
3   Anchor clusters with a main piece
4   Ideally, a single large piece will bring scale

5   Occupy high ceilings with large art and pendant lights
6   Avoid placing objects haphazardly
7   To make low ceilings feel higher, use low furniture and tall artwork
8   Avoid leading the eye upwards towards the ceiling

Calendars Telling the passage of time in a more universal way than a clock, a calendar is best placed in a location where you want to be reminded of the day and the inevitability of forward motion.

Photos of family members Photos of our loved ones are important symbols of unity. Place photos of people, especially family, in frames sitting on side tables close to you, almost as if they were sitting with you. Hanging family portraits high up, though, turns the portraits into a showcase, and puts pressure on you to relive happy family moments. Formally hung portraits are more suitable for deceased people. Never hang photos of people above a fire or active fireplaces.

Lighting Striking, well-designed wall lights may behave like wall art. Note how the lighting reflects off the wall, as the light and shadow it creates may form a strong pattern.

Cuttings, postcards and sticky notes In feng shui, all of these are considered clutter that will hinder the flow of your thoughts, so never place them on the wall. If you must display notes and mementos in this way, invest in a single corkboard, hang that on the wall and confine all notes and so on within its frame.

Artwork When deciding where to place art, consider the subject. Images of landscapes behave like windows, pictures of figures and people are more like mirrors, while graphical art has the same effect as architectural features (such as mouldings) and adds interest to a space. Generally portraits and faces have the greatest ability to draw your eye, so use them thoughtfully.

Words and text Displayed on your walls, these tell you what to think and give little room for interpretation, so consider them carefully. Words can be very forward and might adjust your thoughts over time.

SCULPTURE AND OBJECTS

Unlike wall art, which is representational, objects have their own presence. They occupy the same space as you and I would. As we invite them into our world, so they invite us into theirs. Because they are three-dimensional objects, we can hold, touch and observe them, and be reminded of the moment we first felt them in our hands.

Object types

Objects, apart from sculptures, usually have a purpose – vases, trinket boxes or grandfather clocks, say – which means that many of them already have a specific placement in the home, according to their use.

<u>Vases and vessels</u> Place these in the centre of a table or by a sideboard or table. Always fill them with beautiful contents (flowers or fruit, say) in order that they perform their function.

<u>Lamps</u> Place these only where you need light (see pages 145–151).

<u>Sculpture and ornaments</u> Of course, there are times when we buy objects purely for ornament – porcelain figurines, carved objects, souvenirs from the natural world or a holiday. These will have a theme or design, so place them in an appropriate location in the home that reflects their story. Remember, buy only things that you love and feel passionate about – do not buy objects to act as 'filler' ornamentation.

Some objects are seen as feng shui 'cures' for spaces – things that you buy and place in needy corners of the home to spark certain emotions. The most famous example is the lucky beckoning cat (the *maneki neko*), which originated in Japan, rather than China. Usually decorated heavily in sparkling greens or golds, the cat waves its paw, suggesting that fortune should come its way and into your home. Of course, this does not mean that money will fly through your door, but its presence, both reverent and cute, can be reassuring, and can cure a feeling that something is lacking. But this is dependent on how you feel, which is why you cannot prescribe these things. It all depends on your own beliefs.

The following is a list of some common feng shui items – remember, they are symbols and will not perform miracles!

Ba gua mirror This is a hostile item used to reflect bad incoming chi directly back to its sender. Never hang one inside your home. Rather, hang it outside over an external door. However, I recommend against using it at all – it's an unfriendly gesture.

Calabash gourd Used to absorb bad energies, the calabash gourd may be a better alternative to the ba gua mirror. For example, if your bed is placed against a wall shared with a toilet, you may place a gourd in the space between.

Coins Most obviously representing wealth and fortune, coins in fact have several interesting uses. For example, placing a particular number of coins under the foundations of the entrance to a home is said to bring good fortune into the home.

Dragons These powerful creatures represent the wood element of growth and prosperity. They have very high energy levels, so avoid placing them in calm areas such as the bedroom or bathroom, and place them in the living room instead.

Frog Money frogs are greedy animals who hoard piles of gold coins, and will hold on to wealth for their owners. Never place a frog at the entrance to your home, where there is too much chi. The frog's personality is more private than that of the maneki neko (see opposite).

Fu dogs These popular ornaments usually guard the entrance to a home and must be placed in pairs of male and female. Place the female to your right and the male to your left if you are looking outwards (this is similar to the positioning of the male dragon of the east and female tiger of the west in the cosmic animal assembly).

Fu Lu Shou A trio of deities. Fu represents wealth, Lu represents status and Shou represents longevity.

Mandarin ducks These always come in pairs of a male and a female and present a lovely image of two ducks with different qualities brought together to signify love. Place them in a space in which you want love to flourish.

Ship A sailing ship is said to represent a smooth sailing journey, and also symbolically carries wealth. It should be pointed towards the home to draw wealth in.

Turtle The turtle represents stability. Place it in the rear of your home to signify the mountain that protects your home from behind. This is the only item that you can replace with an actual live animal – although be sure to treat it kindly!

Appliances

Sometimes we have functional appliances, such as home assistants, toasters and kettles, that occupy worktop space. Choose these based on design as well as functionality, even if it's as simple as choosing a colour to match the room. Remember to place appliances where they belong – for example, things intended for food preparation should stay in the kitchen. It may be convenient to have a fridge or a microwave in the bedroom, particularly if you live in a shared house, but keeping functions consistent and appropriate will improve your wellbeing.

Religious objects

Feng shui does not dictate where to place items that command the utmost respect. However, it's common practice to place them in the most important room in the house, which in feng shui terms would be the living room. Avoid the bedroom, as religious objects and the bedroom have wildly different energies. Even if you place them outside the bedroom, do not align the religious objects with the bed. Never put religious objects on the ground, and follow any other advice that your religion may give.

Paper and boxes

These are not worthy objects, so store them out of sight in a methodical way, especially papers. If you are not using the papers any more, throw them away, otherwise they become clutter and hinder the flow of energy in your home.

ITEMS THAT PRODUCE MOVEMENT AND SOUND

Of the many objects in a home, some move and create sound, which bring yang and energy into a room. Imagine a room that is uninhabited, perhaps your bedroom when you're away on a long, long holiday. The room becomes stale. One way to keep it alive without plants or an aquarium is to have a sculpture that moves.

Moving objects

○ Mobiles are all about movement. They sway gently and give a feeling of calm through their gentle gestures.

○ Other moving objects, such as lava lamps, radiometers and windmills, are good for any space – although if the object moves uncontrollably at night, avoid placing it in your bedroom.

- Wind chimes create lovely sounds, and in their chimes are said to absorb energy. In feng shui, wind chimes help to absorb and slow down chi, so place them where there are too many windows, or in thoroughfares, such as a staircase in front of the main door. Never hang them above your bed or your desk. Hollow wind chimes are best, as they allow energy to flow through.

HOW TO USE OBJECTS AND ART

As we've seen, objects and art influence a room, and, if we use them properly, can shape a room in a positive way.

How to display objects

Small things Group small objects in larger, interrelated clusters to have more visual presence, or place them within a display cabinet, which in turn becomes its own larger object. Then have some negative space around them.

Large things These can be standalone ornaments or sculptures. Pair them with items of other scales.

How to display pictures

Small pictures Hang small pictures over furniture pieces, such as sideboards or cabinets. If you have a larger wall, hang them in clusters or grids with a single anchor image in the centre of the cluster. The general height of each composition should be eye level. If the furniture is too high to achieve this, do not hang anything over it.

Large pictures Hang these centrally over a low piece of furniture, or centrally in a prominent wall. The height of the image should be such that it is roughly eye level.

Scale Items on the wall do not actually take up physical space, but give the impression of scale. This is why the general rule is that if you want to make a space feel bigger, you should use bigger artwork. This will work only with objects that you hang – if you cover an entire wall with a mural, the mural becomes part of the room, and will not give the same sense of scale.

Height To heighten ceilings, use tall, narrow artworks (in portrait format). The vertical, rectangular frame evokes the wood element. Tall lamps or sculptures can extend the height of a ceiling as well. You can use these instead of tall plants.

Length To widen a room, use horizontal, landscape pictures, which reference the earth element. You can place long centrepieces on dining tables to give a sense of length, too.

Circular objects Objects such as round artworks or clocks have the same condensing qualities as metal, and draw the eye towards the centre. Hang these symmetrically over an object such as a fireplace. A circular object, such as a round fruit bowl or bulbous vase, in the middle of a coffee table provides a strong anchoring factor.

Other shapes Triangular and wavy, irregular wall pieces are less common, but they refer back to their respective elements, such as fire and water.

Colour If you're afraid of painting your walls colours other than white, place colourful objects around the room in the form of hanging art, sculptures or even throws. However, practise restraint: keep the composition balanced and complementary. The colourfulness of a space is less about the variety of colours you have, and more about the contrast between each colour.

MIRRORS AND CRYSTALS

Mirrors reflect and crystals refract, and both have the ability to control light. Light and movement, as we know, are a source of energy, and being able to control, filter and divert this energy gives mirrors and crystals the potential to change spaces.

○ Unlike pictures, mirrors reflect life – they're not static or interpretive, they're more like windows and doors. Do not place mirrors where you don't want movement chi to come through – particularly around beds and *especially* not at the foot of a bed.

○ In places where there is very little movement, mirrors reflect any motion. Often this movement comes from the person in the room – you – which creates a parallel energy. That's why it's best to avoid placing mirrors in rooms where you want calm, but it's good to place them where you need to inject life.

○ Mirrors double whatever they reflect, so position them so that they reflect the good and not where they might reflect the bad. For example, mirrors in an open-plan kitchen should not reflect the stove, but could reflect the dining table.

○ A mirror can expand the space. This is not just about making a space feel bigger: if your room (other than a bedroom) is missing a corner, place a mirror there to extend and complete the room shape, creating a more auspicious, regular shape overall.

○ Shiny black surfaces, such as TVs, give a similar energy to mirrors, so treat them in the same way.

Mirrors are particularly useful in these locations:

○ High-energy areas, such as the living room.

○ Where there are prosperous items that you want to double, such as food on a dining table.

○ A working environment that places you in a vulnerable position (to give you a view of the door).

○ Any stale room that needs an injection of life.

Avoid using mirrors in these locations:

○ Low-energy areas, such as a bedroom. (If you must have a mirror, ensure you can't see it from your bed.)

○ Outside your home.

○ Long corridors, unless you're reflecting sideways.

○ Areas, such as kitchens, with hostile energy. (If you do have a mirror in your kitchen, avoid positioning it so that it reflects the hob or stove.)

The qualities of your mirror

○ A mirror must have a regular shape and be able to reflect your full image without any gaps, which means it should also be tall and high enough to reflect your face.

○ Choose a mirror that is clean, with no cracks and no distortions.

○ Do not use divided mirrors, such as mirrored tiles.

○ Be aware that concave mirrors can absorb bad energy and convex mirrors can expand energy without reflecting it.

How and where to hang your mirror

○ Do not hang a mirror too high or it will make you feel ungrounded.

○ A mirror that's hung too low will force you to bend down to see your reflection, which can make you feel suppressed.

○ Use mirrors to reflect light and bring chi in to deep, dark corners.

○ If your mirror sits on an angled wall, be mindful of what it will reflect.

○ Avoid positioning a mirror behind you, which will make you feel vulnerable to other people watching you over your shoulder.

168

CRYSTALS

Crystals come in two forms: clear, multi-faceted glass-like objects, or hewn mineral rocks. They can't magically change your life. In fact, apart from jade, they were not commonly used to any effect in classical feng shui. While there is no proven science on how mineral crystals can directly affect our health and fortune, it is undeniable that they have a powerful visual presence – and that can affect how we feel and our wellbeing. The real power of crystals comes from within you – think of them as a reminder of your aspirations and a visual stimulus to enhance your mood.

Clear crystals

These are almost like mirrors. Always keep them clean and sparkling and they will serve to reflect and disperse light, creating beautiful rainbows across the room.

How to hang clear crystals

- Where there is excessive chi, such as at doorways that open on to staircases or beds, hang crystals to disperse light and energy.

- In stagnant areas, such as windowless rooms, crystals bring movement and energy.

- Crystals in the middle of tables or consoles draw in energy.

Mineral crystals

These come in all shapes, sizes, colours and textures. You can wear them on a pendant around your neck or in a bracelet or ring, display them in your home (by hanging them or placing them in a cabinet or on a console, say) or even keep them hidden from view.

<u>Choosing a mineral crystal</u> Broadly, mineral crystals represent earth and your connection to it, but jade is the only stone or crystal traditionally used in feng shui. It has two forms: jadeite and nephrite. While it comes in other colours (ranging from white to orange), a rich, translucent green is its best-known and most coveted hue and is the reason why jade represents the wood element. This, in turn, represents growth and prosperity. You can wear jade in pieces of jewellery, but if you choose to display it in your home, place it in areas where you want to evoke wood.

For all other crystals, observe their visual qualities and focus on how they make you feel before deciding which to position in a space.

WATER

Feng shui means wind and water. While wind serves as a metaphor to describe the environment, water is actually about water, an important element that brings life. As we learned at the beginning of the book, traditional feng shui masters used to place cities and homes on sites close to natural, clean, flowing water, because water is sustenance, trade and wealth, and took away waste. Now, of course, we have the ability to construct our own water sources – but we should respect the power of water all the same.

BRINGING WATER INTO YOUR HOME

○ Water should always be trickling or moving – stagnant water is never good as it signifies stillness and decay, and it is where things like mould or mosquitoes breed.

○ Water destroys when it is in the wrong position, so avoid having water in unnatural locations. In an ideal situation, there should be a flowing river at the entrance of the home, some way down a slope – close enough to bring life, but away from the door and low enough so that it does not pose a risk like flooding or landslides.

○ Never have water in unnatural locations. For example, water above you may symbolise leaks or flooding – I wouldn't advise building a swimming pool on the roof, if you are fortunate enough to have the option! (However, always reflect on the specific situation. There is a building in Hong Kong that is the shape of a cigarette. A feng shui master suggested that they place a pool at the very top to extinguish the fire of the cigarette, because the risk of fire was considered worse than the drawbacks of overhead stagnant water.)

○ You can position a water feature inside an entrance, but contain it so that it will not spill.

○ Water represents wealth, making it a positive feature for places where we work, such as offices and study rooms. However, if you work in your bedroom, adding water will bring too much energy, so avoid any water there.

TYPES OF WATER FEATURE

Water features come in several different forms – swimming pools, ponds, aquariums, fish bowls and fountains among them. These all have different benefits, so consider which one will work for you.

Pools

Swimming pools are particularly unnatural, as they do not carry life or bring trade and wealth. Instead, they are just vessels for water. If possible, you want your pool to have some visible movement, like a waterfall that keeps the water circulating. Always keep the water clean and filtered – if you don't think you can maintain a pool, do not have one!

Ponds

Ponds are better than swimming pools as they are natural ecosystems with fish, plants and life, and have good chi. In the traditional *si he yuan* courtyard house in ancient China, there was always a vessel of water containing fish placed in the middle of the central courtyard. This not only symbolised fortune, but the residents could use it if ever the home caught fire. As with a swimming pool, always keep the water in your pond healthy.

Aquariums and fish bowls

When you do not have a large home, the best source of water is an aquarium or fish bowl. The rule for this is simple: keep it healthy and happy, by removing dead plants and animals, and keeping the water clean. Remember to avoid putting an aquarium or fish bowl in a bedroom.

Fountains

Although fountains are purely ornamental, and do not contain life, the splashes and sprays create movement. Ideally, direct the flow of water towards your home. If your fountain is outside your home, water flowing inwards represents wealth, which is why in Asia you often see unusual upward- and inward-spouting fountains in front of office buildings.

However, if you have a small fountain inside your home, there is no guide to how it should flow, simply that the motion of the water should be calming and trickling.

ALTERNATIVES TO WATER

Of course, it's not necessary to have actual water flowing in your home to attract fortune. If you live in a dry, arid place, plants offer the same assurance of wealth as does water. This is because plants represent the element wood, which can exist only where water is present, too. If you do not wish to have plants, try shiny blue, glazed tiles or pottery, which (with the ripply, reflective surface) create the impression of water.

Finally, you could opt for images of water, which will help to bring the element into your space. Use calming images of lakes or waterfalls, rather than images of stormy seas.

INDOOR
PLANTS

This section focuses on plants that are good for interiors. Unlike art or accessories, plants are living, breathing beings and have more life chi than any ornament – even more than motifs of dragons! Perhaps surprisingly, as long as all your plants are happy, having lots of them in your home will not give overwhelming chi, because they are natural. Plants also have specific feng shui uses and symbolism – but their influence depends on how they look, and where you have positioned them inside your home.

WHEN DO YOU NEED PLANTS?

In most cases, looking out on to a garden or some greenery is enough to bring a balance of wood into a space – so if you don't like caring for plants, you don't need to have them. (The first rule is that you must be able to care for plants. It's better to have no plants at all, than to have dead plants!)

But, if your view has no greenery, your home might feel like a shell with no soul. In this case you'll need plants to bring life.

REASONS TO USE PLANTS INDOORS

○ To hide sharp corners in the wall.

○ To soften windows with too much light.

○ To bring life to yin areas – although remember plants still need light to grow.

○ To add the element of wood to enliven earth rooms.

○ To soften the straightness of long corridors.

WHERE TO LOCATE INDOOR PLANTS

While plants really belong outside, you can keep them inside in the right conditions. When considering where to position indoor plants, always think about their natural, outdoor habitat. If your home is dark, consider plants that naturally need less light, such as ground-layer rainforest plants.

Entrances Plants are particularly good for the entry area of a home, as they show that your home is located on fertile ground where life will flourish. That said, hallways, especially in apartments, are often far from the windows, so if your plant will not survive, it's better to do without.

Bedrooms Avoid having plants in your bedroom. When finding a place to settle and rest, you're looking for a spot that's safe from the elements. The presence of plants signifies the presence of water and light, and of energy – and the bedroom is a place that should be dark and dry, and so restful. In addition, plants compete for oxygen at night when they respire, so they will share your air. Of course, feng shui can provide only a guide: if you regard plants as your friends, and they help you feel calm, follow that feeling and by all means have them in your bedroom. If you do this, place them in a single cluster, immediately beside the window. This mimics their natural behaviour, gathering together in the most fertile ground, and it places them close to the opening of your room. Then, position your bed as far as you can from your mini garden. You can also make an exception for hospital beds: as there is so much yin in hospitals, plants introduce a good balance of yang and life.

Living and dining areas As living rooms are places of positive energy and plants represent life and chi, this makes a great match. Nonetheless, avoid scattering plants all over these spaces. Instead, form clusters located close to the windows.

Study and offices Plants in work areas signify growth and prosperity. However, if your desk is in your bedroom, keep the plants further away from the bed. Usually in such situations, your desk would be located close to the window, which is also better for the plant.

Kitchen Plants signify the wood element, which in the kitchen helps to alleviate the heat from cooking, and mediate fire and water, which are usually both present. Avoid placing your plants too close to the stove, as wood feeds fire.

Bathroom Wood (from plants) leads on to the water element in the bathroom. This means that a plant in a bathroom is a good pairing.

The bathroom is also a humid place where some species thrive, but you should have plants there only if your bathroom has windows to offer natural light.

TYPES OF PLANT

The best plants are full and luscious with broad green leaves. In feng shui, plants are about their appearance rather than their species, as the colour green symbolises the wood element and growth, and, of course, it is the colour of jade (see pages 169–70).

<u>Large leafy plants</u> These plants – including money plants, monsteras and peperomias, which have big, green, roundish leaves – are the best types for your home. They bring rich tones of deep green, while being full and luscious with rounded non-aggressive leaf shapes. You can place these plants anywhere.

<u>Ferns with soft green foliage</u> While ferns may have pointed leaves, their soft structure plays down these harsh shapes, and their nature suggests that your home is fertile.

<u>Succulents with rounded leaves</u> Cacti are not generally recommended for the home (see page 180), but some types – with bulgy, rounded leaves, such as jade plants or echeverias – are welcome. Avoid aloe vera, or other cacti with pointed leaves.

<u>The Four Gentlemen</u> Chinese culture specifically upholds four notable plants, known as the Four Gentlemen, which symbolise the seasons and celebrate the virtues that each represents during those times:

178

GOOD

Choose soft, leafy plants in vivid colours, as these represent abundance and life.

BAD

Dead plants never look good. Avoid thorny or spiky plants as they are visually more hostile.

○ The hardy yet graceful orchid represents spring taking hold.

○ The strength and growth of bamboo represents summer in full energy.

○ The chrysanthemum represents virtue and growth for the transitional season of autumn. Note that chrysanthemums also represent death and are common funeral flowers.

○ Plum blossom, with its demure resilience, represents hope in winter.

TYPES OF PLANT TO THINK TWICE ABOUT

Just to be clear, there's no such thing as a 'bad plant', but when using plants indoors, there are always considerations to make. Plants come in various shapes and sizes, and some of them, such as cacti (with their spiky thorns) and palms (with spiky leaves or needles), have a more aggressive appearance than others. Look for visual cues and make the right associations for your spaces.

Cacti Noted for their sharp, pointy spikes, cacti are among the few plants that are not recommended for inside the home. This is not only because of their aggressive appearance, but because they signify arid and inhospitable climates. They are fine outside of the home and even represent protection.

Succulents with pointed leaves These pointed leaves symbolise fire more than wood. While they are more acceptable in the home than cacti, place them only in places that can take this more aggressive appearance and the element of fire.

Snake plants These plants have straight, pointed leaves, which appear aggressive and reflect the fire element more than they reflect wood. However, their powerful shapes suggest upward growth and shield you from bad chi. You can place them in your home, but treat them as a fire element, avoiding them in calming areas.

Palms and dracenas Beautiful plants with generally pointed leaves, these are acceptable in the home – depending on the precise leaf shape. If their leaves are soft and flowing downwards, they represent wood and water. If they are like upward bursts of pointed leaves, the plant is linked to wood and fire. Place these plants according to the feelings you wish to achieve in a room – usually a higher energy area, such as a living space or a kitchen.

Fake plants

Avoid fake plants as much as possible, because they spell an imbalance of the environment. This is true even if you have a basement space with no access to light; having a plastic plant will just look wrong. Fake plants do not renew and regenerate, which means they will collect dust and cobwebs. If you prefer not to care for plants, use other ornaments or features instead (see below).

Dead plants

Needless to say, feng shui advises against keeping dead plants. Some dead plants may be beautiful – dried hydrangeas or eucalyptus, for example – and these are more acceptable than plants that have simply died through lack of care or nourishment. Avoid them when you can, nonetheless.

Plant alternatives

If you aren't able to successfully grow plants in your space, replace them with ornaments that suggest life and growth – hanging mobiles, sculptural lights or even feathers are all good choices. A large and full bowl of fruit can have the same rejuvenating effect as having plants in the house. Do not attempt to paint something green, which will feel artificial.

GARDENS AND BALCONIES

Building placement is the fundamental preoccupation of feng shui, so if you can, sculpt the landscape around your home in the most positive, feng-shui-friendly ways possible. As plants can shape the landscape and environment, using them strategically in your outdoor areas can have a rather powerful impact on your health and wellbeing.

SCULPTING THE LANDSCAPE

If you're lucky enough to have a garden, design it to encourage a healthy flow of chi around your home, using the placement of plants, pathways and structures to help you.

Imagine your garden is a room inside the house. First, it should have a main centrepiece – perhaps a fountain, gazebo, bench or even a useful clearing. Then, plan your pathways round this centrepiece to allow a good flow of chi. Note any places where you will sit and rest, and give them the qualities of command positions.

Design your garden to be a functional space that will extend the functions of your home. Place higher plants and trees at the very rear of the garden to enclose and protect you.

If your home is irregular in shape with missing corners, use your garden to sculpt it. If you want to include a water feature, include one to the front of the house (see page 52), but ideally not behind.

The classic command position

<u>Tortoise</u> The classic tortoise position means to have a mountain or slope behind your house. It's particularly good if you can have an actual mound behind the house, although it can be hard to find plots with hills behind them. Planting tall and dense trees at the back of the house can give the same effect as the mound. The shapes of trees reference the silhouettes of mountains: the rounded and more sinuous tops of sculpted trees or bushes are more yin and gentle; jagged shapes, like those of pine trees or palms, are stronger and more yang.

<u>Bird</u> The front of the house should be the classic bird position, which is open to view, but at the same time not completely exposed. Low bushes and meandering pathways here create a calming approach that offers some privacy and space between the outside world and the house. If you have a long and straight driveway leading directly to the house, place a roundabout (such as a tub with growing flowers) to block any aggressive chi from rushing in.

Pathways

The way you design pathways in your garden alters the speed of chi that flows around it. Any pathways that lead to the door should be gently curved, just like pathways in nature.

BALCONIES AND COURTYARDS

Balconies and courtyards are important spaces, especially for apartments or homes in the city. They allow you to step outside and connect with the environment, and are an extension of the home.

Never leave your balcony or courtyard barren and grey. Even if the space is tiny, it's worth giving up some of what you have to create a natural and protected environment. Then, add function to the space – consider placing versatile furniture there, such as seats or a dining table. Plan your space so that you can walk around your furniture. If you have a balcony, clear a space so that you can access the edge of it to enjoy the view – whether that view is good or bad!

Good views

A good view links your home with the world outside – so don't obscure it. Avoid hanging anything in front of a view, and place moderate, low-lying plants that you can look over, or position taller ones to the side to frame the view without blocking it.

Bad views

If your view is poor (perhaps you look out on a harsh concrete landscape), use your balcony to soften it. Don't be tempted to block it, because you need the light. Instead, place lots of lush plants on your balcony to draw the attention inwards.

Cherish the outdoor space

If you need to fix the internal layout of your home (perhaps because the balcony doorway happens to be the command position for your sofa), never be tempted to block off your access to your outside space. However bad the feng shui of a room may be, closing off a balcony or courtyard to fix it will only make things worse, creating dead space outside. Remember that your balcony or courtyard is an extension of your main living space, rather than separate from it. Plan the furniture placement in the room so that you can look out and easily access your outdoor space.

Note from Cliff Outdoor space is an important way in which we connect with nature, but some apartments do not have such spaces. Instead, use other means to create this connection within your home. Choose furniture that encourages you to spend time by a window. For example, consider placing an open bench or daybed under a window, giving you the choice to sit facing either into the living area, or out towards the views outside.

If you can safely leave them there, place plants on sills and ledges. This will let you frame views with soft foliage to soften the chi and harsh light that enters your space. If your windows have no windowsills or they are floor-to-ceiling glass, simply place plants close to the windows to create a transitioning space between inside and out.

6

Endnote

CONCLUSION

Congratulations for making all the way to the end of this book!

Feng shui is about making the most of your spaces, no matter how awkward or small, regardless of whether you rent or own. Now that you've read about the principles and see how to apply them, I hope that feng shui no longer feels mysterious, but rather like the sensible approach that it is. With feng shui, you can create a better home – and this can change your life.

It took me some time to understand the power of feng shui myself. I am from Singapore, where – like in most east Asian cities – almost all homes are built in new, regularised tower blocks. There is little variation or choice to spaces, and I didn't really think about needing to apply feng shui until I moved to London to become an architect in 2010.

I still remember the day I arrived. My first home was a tiny trapezoid-shaped attic room on Sandwich Street with a broken window; I immediately felt a sense of oppression from the walls sloping in on me and barged out in panic. I had never felt this way before! But rather than moving out, I came back with a purpose: I was going to transform this room by shifting the furniture around according to the principles of feng shui. It was the first time I had truly felt the effects of this practice. Since then, I have applied the principles of feng shui to every project I've worked on. My puzzled clients have never known why their homes have felt so good – until now.

Feng shui has always been a knowledge that was passed down. Much of what I know came from my grandfather, and with this book I hope to share my knowledge, just as it was shared with me, many years ago. Now you've read the book, you can also pass it along to your friends and family.

So now you know!

GLOSSARY

	USA	UK	AUSTRALIA
ROOMS	apartment	flat	apartment
	bathroom	toilet	bathroom
	den	snug	family room
	foyer	entrance	lobby (or foyer, or entry)
	great room	drawing room	rumpus room
	living room	sitting room	lounge room
	TV room	lounge	family room
	walk-in closet	walk-in wardrobe	walk-in wardrobe
FIXTURES, FITTINGS AND FURNITURE	closet	wardrobe	wardrobe
	couch or sofa	sofa	couch or sofa
	dresser	chest of drawers	chest of drawers
	elevator	lift	lift
	full bed	double bed	double bed
	hood	extractor	rangehood
	nightstand	bedside table	bedside table
	stove	cooker	stove
	toilet	WC/toilet	toilet
	trash can	dustbin	bin
	twin bed	single bed	single bed

ACKNOWLEDGEMENTS

I would like to thank TikTok for helping me realise that feng shui is an appreciated artform, and Lauren Whybrow for discovering me, and bringing this book to fruition.

ABOUT THE AUTHOR

Cliff Tan is a graduate of the Architectural Association School of Architecture, and his practice combines architecture with feng shui. Cliff has over one million followers on TikTok, and his explanatory videos on feng shui have been viewed millions of times. Cliff was born in Singapore, and now lives in London. This is his first book.

ABOUT THE ILLUSTRATOR

Dura Lee is a South Korean illustrator who lives in Seoul. She originally studied fashion, before becoming an artist. Her most recent graphic novel, *Youth and Island*, was released in 2020.

BLOOMSBURY PUBLISHING
Bloomsbury Publishing Plc
50 Bedford Square, London, WC1B 3DP, UK
29 Earlsfort Terrace, Dublin 2, Ireland

BLOOMSBURY, BLOOMSBURY PUBLISHING and the Diana logo
are trademarks of Bloomsbury Publishing Plc

First published in Great Britain 2022

A catalogue record for this book is available from the British Library

Library of Congress Cataloguing-in-Publication data has been applied for

ISBN: HB: 978-1-5266-3999-8; eBook: 978-1-5266-4000-0

10 9 8 7 6 5 4 3 2 1

Editor: Lauren Whybrow
Copyeditor: Judy Barratt
Designer and typesetters: Evi-O.Studio | Nicole Ho and Evi O.
Production Manager: Laura Brodie
Illustrator: Dura Lee

Printed in China by C&C Offset Printing Co. Ltd

To find out more about our authors and books visit www.bloomsbury.com
and sign up for our newsletters